Lightning Kite Snow Fur Open Horse Rat Net Duck Oil Get Orange River Frog Later Cloud Flower Shell Seed Internet Joke Earth Juice Planets Honey In Long Rain Milk Globe Key Hospital

A note for parents

This comprehensive dictionary is specially designed for inquisitive children who are eager to learn new words and their meanings.

All their favourite Disney characters are on hand throughout the book to guide your child on an amazing journey of discovery. Each word is accompanied by a fun picture, a helpful definition and a sentence to put the word into context.

Why not set your child off on a learning adventure by introducing three new words a day? Your child could learn three new words every day for almost a year!

My First
Picture
Dictionary

This edition published by Parragon Books Ltd in 2014

Parragon Books Ltd
Chartist House
15–17 Trim Street
Bath BA1 1HA, UK
www.parragon.com

ISBN 978-1-4454-6546-3

Printed in China

My First
Picture
Dictionary

Learning is fun with your Disney friends

PaRRagon

Bath • New York • Singapore • Hong Kong • Cologne • Delhi
Melbourne • Amsterdam • Johannesburg • Shenzhen

apple

accident

An accident is something that happens by mistake.

Only Goofy could have an **accident** like that!

acorn

An acorn is the hard nut of the oak tree.

The **acorn** is Chip 'n' Dale's favourite food!

above

When you are above something, you are on top of it or higher than it.

It's fun to fly **above** the clouds!

act

To act is to pretend to be something that you're not.

Baloo is trying to **act** like an orang-utan!

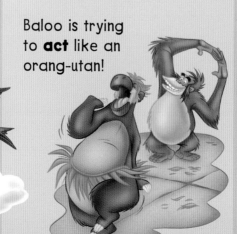

action

An action is something that is done.

Mushu can learn a lot from watching Mulan in **action,** doing karate.

actor

An actor is a person who makes believe he or she is someone else in a film, a play or a television show.

Donald thinks he is a great **actor**.

adult

An adult is someone who has grown up.

Simba, you're a cub now, but soon you'll be an **adult** lion!

add

When you add something, you put it with something else.

Let's **add** more coins to my collection!

adventure

An adventure is something you do that is new and exciting.

Wendy and her brothers had quite an **adventure**, flying with Peter Pan!

after

After means later than, or following.

The toys are all in a row **after** Andy's mum cleans.

address

An address tells the location of a building or the place where someone lives. It can include a number, street, city, county and country.

Let's check the **address** to see where the letter is going!

aeroplane

An aeroplane is a flying machine with wings that can carry people a long way.

An **aeroplane** is the fastest way to travel!

afternoon

Afternoon means after 12 o'clock (noon).

Lady and Tramp run in the park every **afternoon**.

A
B
C
D
E
F
G
H
I
J
K
L
M
N
O
P
Q
R
S
T
U
V
W
X
Y
Z

A
B
C
D
E
F
G
H
I
J
K
L
M
N
O
P
Q
R
S
T
U
V
W
X
Y
Z

agree

When people agree, it means they think or feel the same way about something.

Let's **agree** to play with everything!

alarm clock

An alarm clock has a buzzer or bell that wakes you up.

Donald wakes up right away when his **alarm clock** goes off!

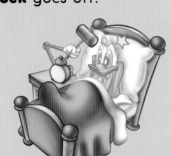

alien

An alien is a living creature from another planet.

Hmm. Earth might be a good place for an **alien** to hide!

airport

An airport is a place where aeroplanes take off and land.

The **airport** is very busy!

all

All means every part of something.

All my hands are full! How many hands do you have?

alone

You are alone when you are by yourself.

When Lilo is **alone,** she likes to listen to her Elvis records.

also

Also means as well as, in addition to.

Cinderella **also** sings while she cleans.

amusement park

An amusement park is a place with rides and food where people go to have fun.

I can see the whole **amusement park**!

answer

An answer is what you give after a question is asked.

Scuttle, you'll know the **answer**! What is this thing?

always

Always means all the time.

Baloo **always** scratches his back against a tree!

angry

When you get cross, you feel angry.

Calm down, you two! Don't be so **angry** with each other!

ant

An ant is a tiny, crawling insect that is very strong.

Flik is a small **ant** with big ideas!

ambulance

An ambulance is a van with a siren that takes sick people to the hospital.

Cars move to the side of the road to let an **ambulance** pass.

animal

An animal is any living thing that is not a plant.

Mufasa is an **animal** that lives in the jungle.

apple

An apple is the fruit that grows on an apple tree.

The evil Witch gave Snow White a poisoned **apple**!

apron

An apron is something to wear that protects your other clothing when you cook.

It's okay if you spill something (by accident) on your **apron**.

around

Around means on all sides of something.

Simba chases Nala **around** the tree.

audience

An audience is a group of people watching something.

The Aristocats enjoy making music for an **audience** of any size!

aquarium

An aquarium is a bowl or tank of water that holds fish and other sea creatures.

This cat can only watch the fish in the **aquarium**.

ask

When you ask something, you use words to form a question.

May I **ask** you to read to me?

aunt

An aunt is a sister of your father or mother, or the wife of your uncle.

I love being your **Aunt** Daisy!

armchair

An armchair is a big, comfortable chair with arms.

I like sitting in a comfy **armchair** when I read a good book!

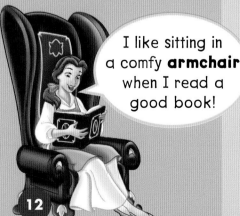

astronaut

An astronaut is someone who travels into outer space.

An **astronaut** wears a special suit.

autumn

Autumn is one of the four seasons of the year. It is when the leaves change colour and fall off the trees.

Yummy acorns fall in the **autumn**, too!

bear

Bb

backpack

A backpack is a bag that goes over your shoulders and hangs down your back.

Mike takes his **backpack** to university!

badminton

Badminton is a game played by hitting a shuttlecock over a net using raquets.

Badminton is a really fun sport!

bacon

Bacon is smoked meat that is sliced and fried.

Bacon smells so good when it's cooking!

bag

A bag is a soft container used to carry things.

We can carry our shopping home in a **bag**.

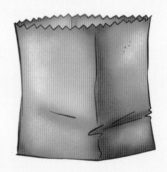

baby

A baby is a very young child.

What a curious-looking **baby**!

bad

When something is bad, it is not good.

Lucifer is a **bad** cat!

bake

When you bake something, you cook it in an oven.

I'll be happy to **bake** that pie for you!

baker's shop

A baker's shop is a place that sells tasty food such as bread, cakes and biscuits.

Mmmm! Smell the fresh bread being made at the **baker's shop**!

balloon

A balloon is a thin rubber bag that is blown up with air or gas.

The red **balloon** belongs to Daisy.

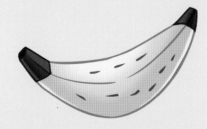

band

A band is a group of musicians who play together.

We're the Under the Sea **Band**!

ball

A ball is a round object that is used to play games.

Let's play catch with the **ball**!

ballerina

A ballerina is a female ballet dancer.

A **ballerina** is usually very graceful.

banana

A banana is a long, yellow fruit that grows on a tree.

Abu can peel a **banana** very quickly to get to the fruit inside!

bandage

A bandage is a strip of cloth used to cover a wound.

It's good to cover a scraped knee with a **bandage**.

bank

A bank is a place where people keep their money.

A monster is standing outside the **bank**.

basketball

Basketball is a game where you throw a large round ball through a raised hoop.

You don't have to be tall to be good at **basketball**!

bank (piggy)

A piggy bank is a toy usually shaped like a pig for you to keep coins in at home.

Huey is proud of all the money he's saved in his **piggy bank**.

bass

The bass is the biggest of the stringed musical instruments.

The Scat Cat Band uses the **bass** when its members play together.

bat

A bat is a flying animal that comes out at night.

Bats are curious animals and they can hang upside down.

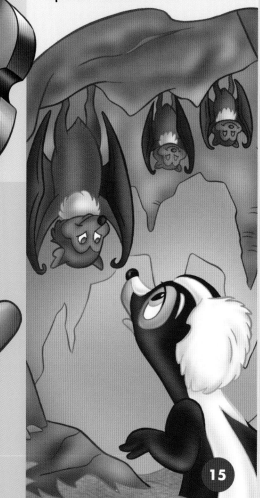

barn

A barn is a building where farm animals live.

Cows and horses are some animals that live in a **barn**.

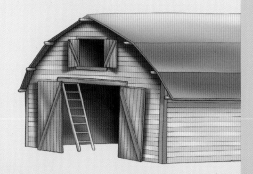

bat

A bat is a stick used to hit a ball.

When it's your turn, keep your eyes on the ball and swing the **bat** at just the right time!

bathtime

When you take a bath – bathtime – you become clean.

*If you don't mind, I like a little privacy at **bathtime**!*

bath

A bath is the thing in which you wash yourself to get clean.

*Playing in the **bath** can be fun!*

beans

Beans are the seeds of different plants.

Beans come in many shapes and colours, such as long and green, or round and white.

bathrobe

A bathrobe is a piece of clothing that you put on after bathtime.

Snuggle up in your warm, comfy **bathrobe**!

be

To be is to live or exist.

*I'm a cute kitten now, and I will **be** a beautiful cat someday!*

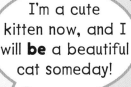

bear

A bear is a big, furry animal that growls when it talks and has sharp teeth and claws.

The only **bear** you should hug is your teddy bear!

bathroom

A bathroom is a room with a sink, bath and often a shower and toilet.

Goofy takes a lot of showers so he can sing in the **bathroom**!

beach

A beach is the sandy or rocky place at the edge of the sea.

*Welcome to my **beach**! Grab a towel and enjoy the sun!*

beard

A beard is the hair that grows on a man's chin and cheeks.

To get King Triton's attention, Sebastian pulls on his **beard**.

bed

A bed is a piece of furniture that you sleep on.

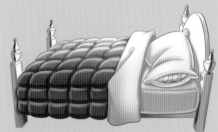

Do you get tucked into **bed** every night?

bee

A bee is a flying insect that lives in a hive.

Bees make lots of yummy honey in their hive.

beautiful

Something beautiful is pleasing to look at.

Cinderella's gown is so **beautiful**!

become

Become means to change or grow into something new.

Sebastian wants to **become** the most honoured bandleader of all time!

bedroom

A bedroom is where you go to sleep at night.

One night, Wendy and her brothers saw a ship outside their **bedroom** window!

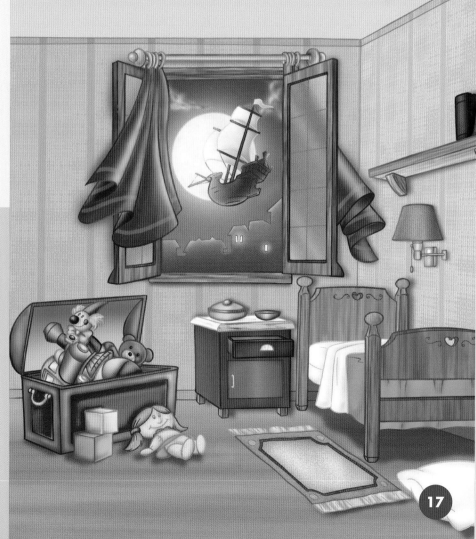

A
B
C
D
E
F
G
H
I
J
K
L
M
N
O
P
Q
R
S
T
U
V
W
X
Y
Z

before

Before means earlier than something else.

The Dwarfs' cottage was messy **before** Snow White moved in.

behind

Behind means at the back of something.

Nala found Simba hiding **behind** the rock.

bell

A bell is a hollow metal object that rings when it is struck.

The **bell** rings every morning when school starts.

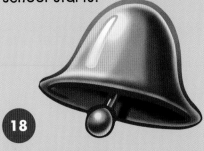

below

Below means under or lower than something else.

Nala! You're above me, and I'm **below** you!

belt

A belt is a long, narrow strip of leather or cloth that you wear around your waist.

Minnie was looking for a red **belt** to wear with her new dress.

bench

A bench is a narrow seat, often found in parks.

This **bench** is a good place to sit and watch the busy park!

best

If something is the best, it means that there is nothing better.

Ariel, you are the **best** singer!

between

To be between something means to be in the middle of other things.

I am standing **between** Thumper and Bambi!

bicycle

A bicycle is something with two wheels, a seat and handlebars; you ride it by pushing on the pedals with your feet.

Donald can't win the race with that **bicycle**!

big

If something is big, it means it takes up a lot of space.

Dumbo's ears are **big**, even for an elephant!

bird

A bird is an animal that has wings and feathers, and lays eggs.

Birds perch in the trees and sing.

birdcage

A birdcage is a container with bars where a pet bird lives.

Only the finest **birdcage** will do for you, my pretty little birdie!

birthday party

A birthday party happens on the day of the year on which you were born.

Huey, Dewey and Louie share one big **birthday party**.

bite

When you bite something, you grab it with your teeth.

Puppies love to **bite** slippers!

blackboard

A blackboard is a hard board on which you write and draw with chalk.

The class uses the schoolroom **blackboard** every day.

blanket

A blanket is a soft cover for a bed.

Daisy loves a big, warm **blanket** to keep her cosy on winter nights.

board game

A board game is a game for two or more players that involves moving pieces around on a board marked with coloured areas.

Mickey loves to play this **board game** with his friends.

A B C D E F G H I J K L M N O P Q R S T U V W X Y Z

boat

A boat carries people and things across the water.

It's fun to take a **boat** ride!

bone

Bones are one of the hard parts of someone's body that all together make up a skeleton. Many animals have bones.

Sniff! Sniff! Pluto's nose knows there's a meat **bone** nearby!

book

A book is something that you read. It has pages and a cover.

Belle reads a **book** every chance she gets.

body

Your body is all of you, inside and outside.

Can you find all the different parts of your **body**?

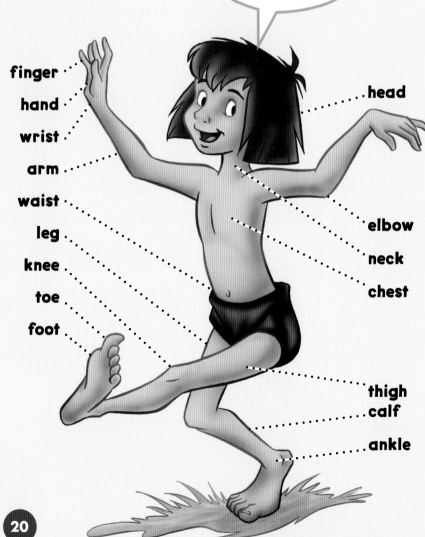

finger

hand

wrist

arm

waist

leg

knee

toe

foot

head

elbow

neck

chest

thigh
calf

ankle

bookcase

A bookcase is a piece of furniture with shelves where you keep books.

Every **bookcase** Belle has is full!

bookshop

A bookshop is a shop that sells books.

This **bookshop** has so many great things to read!

BOOKSHOP

boots

Boots are shoes that cover part of the legs.

Splash! These **boots** will keep your feet dry in puddles!

bottle (baby)

A baby drinks from a special bottle with a teat on it.

When you were a baby, you drank milk from a **bottle**.

bowl

A bowl is a deep, round dish that holds food.

Look at the colourful fruits in the **bowl**!

bored

You are bored when you have nothing interesting to do.

Buzz is so **bored** when he's not with his pal Woody.

bottle

A bottle is a container that holds a liquid.

The Aristocats were given a whole **bottle** of milk as a treat.

box

A box is a container usually in the shape of a square or rectangle.

A pretty **box** like this should hold pretty things!

boring

Something is boring when it doesn't interest you.

Mortie and Ferdie think Mickey is teaching a **boring** subject.

boy

A boy is a child who will grow up to be a man.

John is the oldest **boy** in the Darling household.

bread

Bread is a food made from flour, water and yeast, and is baked.

This **bread** is crusty on the outside and soft on the inside. *Yum!*

bridge

A bridge connects two pieces of land separated by water.

Maid Marian, thank you for this walk across the **bridge**!

break

When you break something, it falls to pieces or stops working.

May hopes her new vase won't **break** like the old one.

bring

When you bring something, you take it with you when you go somewhere.

Garsh! Next time it rains, I'll **bring** a better umbrella!

broccoli

Broccoli is a green vegetable that looks like a little tree.

Broccoli is crunchy when you eat it raw.

breakfast

Breakfast is the first meal of the day.

Donald should eat his **breakfast,** not wear it!

broom

A broom is a long stick with a brush at the end of it that is used for sweeping.

This is an enchanted **broom** – it's carrying buckets of water!

brother

If you have a brother, he is the boy child of your parents.

> Come here, little **brother**. It's time for bed!

butter

Butter is a soft food made from milk or cream.

Mmmm, let's spread the **butter** on fresh, warm bread!

build

When you build something, you make it by putting pieces together.

> What else can I **build** for Belle?

bus

A bus is a long van that carries people from place to place. It has lots of seats and windows.

Let's sit upstairs on the double-decker **bus**!

butterfly

A butterfly is a flying insect that has colourful wings.

A **butterfly** will flutter by in the spring.

building

A building is a place where people live or work. It has walls and a roof.

There are a lot of tall **buildings** in a city.

butcher's shop

A butcher's shop is a shop where people buy meat.

A **butcher's shop** sells chicken, steak and other kinds of meat.

buy

When you buy something, you pay money for it so it can belong to you.

> I will never let you **buy** my Dalmatians!

cat

Cc

café

A café is a place that serves drinks and snacks such as sandwiches and cakes.

You can meet your friends at the **café**.

cake

Cake is a sweet, baked dessert made with flour, sugar, butter and other things.

Minnie baked this **cake** for Daisy's birthday party.

calendar

A calendar lists all the days of the week, month and year.

Hooray, the **calendar** tells me my birthday is on a Saturday!

cabbage

Cabbage is a green vegetable that is boiled or eaten raw.

This **cabbage** looks like a big, green flower!

calculator

A calculator is a machine that can add, subtract, multiply and divide.

I need a **calculator** to count all my Elvis records.

call

Call means to speak in a loud voice to get someone's attention, or to telephone someone.

Minnie loves to **call** her friends.

camel

A camel is an animal that lives in the desert and has one or two humps on its back.

This **camel** is looking for Aladdin. Have you seen him?

candlestick

A candlestick is a holder for a candle.

> I am the brightest **candlestick** of all!

card

A card is a thick piece of paper, often with words and pictures on it.

Minnie got a nice, long **card** from her pen pal.

camera

A camera is a machine that you use to take photographs.

> Smile for the **camera**, Boo!

candyfloss

Candyfloss looks like a cloud on a stick and is made out of spun sugar.

Every good fair has a **candyfloss** stand.

candle

A candle is a stick of wax with a wick that burns and gives you light.

Make a wish and blow out the **candles**!

car

A car is a vehicle with four wheels and an engine that is powered by petrol, diesel or electricity.

Lightning McQueen is a **car** that loves to race!

cardigan

A cardigan is a woolly piece of clothing that buttons up at the front.

Roz is nice and warm in her **cardigan!**

cards

Cards are thick pieces of rectangular paper, with different numbers and shapes on them, that come in a set and are used for games.

Mickey and Donald get together to play **cards** every week.

carry

When you carry something, you hold it to take it with you somewhere.

Daisy helps Donald **carry** her presents.

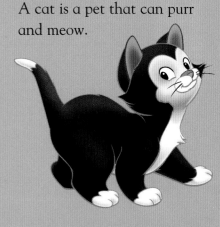

cat

A cat is a pet that can purr and meow.

Figaro is Geppetto's **cat**.

carpet

A carpet is a covering for a floor.

Wow! This **carpet** sure can fly!

catch

When you catch something, you grab it as it is moving.

It's hard to know which ball to **catch** first!

carrot

A carrot is a vegetable that is the long, orange root of a carrot plant.

Bunnies love to eat crunchy **carrots**.

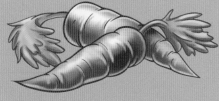

castle

A castle is a large building with thick, stone walls and tall towers.

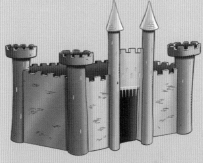

Every princess has at least one **castle** to live in!

cauliflower

A cauliflower is a large, round, bumpy-looking vegetable.

Cauliflower is a vegetable that's white and healthy.

CD (compact disc)

A CD is a disc that plays music and games on a CD player or computer.

Put on a **CD** and let's dance!

cello

A cello is a musical instrument with strings that looks like a huge violin.

That **cello** belongs to the Scat Cat Band.

chalk

Chalk is a stick of coloured powder that you use to write or draw on a blackboard.

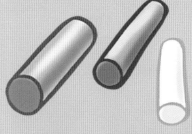

Teachers write on the blackboard with **chalk**.

ceiling

The ceiling is the top part of a room.

It looks as though that ship could touch the **ceiling** if it sailed through the window!

cereal

Cereal is a food you eat for breakfast.

Cereal with milk is a good way to start your day.

chameleon

A chameleon is a small reptile that can change colour.

Pascal the **chameleon** is great at hide-and-seek!

celery

Celery is a crunchy, stringy, green vegetable.

Snap! That's the sound fresh **celery** makes when you break off a piece.

chair

A chair is a piece of furniture to sit on.

Belle sits in a comfy **chair** when she's reading a good book.

champion

A champion is the best person at doing something specific.

When it comes to scaring kids, Sulley is the **champion**!

SCARE TOTALS

1ˢᵗ SULLIVAN

2ⁿᵈ RANDALL

A B C D E F G H I J K L M N O P Q R S T U V W X Y Z

A
B
C
D
E
F
G
H
I
J
K
L
M
N
O
P
Q
R
S
T
U
V
W
X
Y
Z

chase

When you chase something, you try to catch it.

I'm going to **chase** you . . . and catch you!

chess

Chess is a game for two people, played with 32 pieces on a board with light and dark squares.

I am better at **chess** than you are!

children

Two or more young people are called children.

There are three **children** in the Darling family – Wendy, John and Michael.

cheese

Cheese is a food made from the milk of cows, sheep or goats.

Gus just loves **cheese**!

chicken

A chicken is a bird that lays eggs you can eat.

Chickens can't fly very far.

chocolate

Chocolate is a sweet, brown treat made from cocoa beans and sugar.

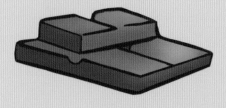

Unwrap a **chocolate** bar and take a big bite!

cherry

A cherry is the fruit that grows on a cherry tree.

A sweet **cherry** is a juicy summer treat.

child

A child is a young person who will grow up to be an adult.

'Children' is the word for more than one **child**.

choose

When you choose something, you pick it out from other things.

Mickey, let's **choose** the perfect tie!

clarinet

A clarinet is a long, thin musical instrument you blow into to make music.

The Scat Cats really swing when they play the **clarinet**!

clean

If something is clean, it is not dirty.

These Dalmatian puppies are all **clean** after their bath.

circus

A circus is a show with clowns and animals.

Step right up and see the greatest flea **circus** in the world!

climb

When you climb, you use your hands and feet to take you higher.

Baloo helps Mowgli **climb** the tree.

clap

You clap your hands together to show you are pleased with something.

Clap, clap! They like Pinocchio's dancing!

classroom

A classroom is the room in a school where a teacher teaches students.

Everyone laughs in Goofy's **classroom**!

A B **C** D E F G H I J K L M N O P Q R S T U V W X Y Z

clock

A clock is a machine that tells us what time it is.

I'm one **clock** that's on time!

clown

A clown is someone in a circus who wears funny clothes and does things to make people laugh.

The dog and the **clown** work together!

coffee

Coffee is a drink made from roasted coffee beans.

Many grown-ups drink **coffee** in the morning.

close

When you close something, such as a door, you shut it.

Donald can't **close** the door against his unwelcome visitor.

coach

A coach is a person who teaches people how to do something better.

This bunch could use a good **coach**!

coin

A coin is a round, metal piece of money.

The only thing Uncle Scrooge likes better than a **coin** is five **coins**!

cloud

A cloud is a white shape in the sky, made up of millions of tiny raindrops.

No two **clouds** are shaped exactly the same.

30

coat

A coat is a piece of clothing you wear over other clothes to keep yourself warm and dry.

Minnie's favourite **coat** has a big, pink flower on it.

cold

When you have a cold, you sneeze a lot and you don't feel well.

Poor Minnie! She has a very bad **cold**!

colours

The way that things reflect light makes them appear in different colours.

Pocahontas sees so many **colours** in nature.

green

orange

yellow

blue

black

purple

red

pink

brown

white

grey

A B C D E F G H I J K L M N O P Q R S T U V W X Y Z

comb

A comb is a flat piece of plastic with teeth that you use to keep your hair neat.

A **comb** feels good going through your hair, doesn't it?

computer

A computer is a machine we type on and do many things with, like writing letters.

Using a **computer** is so easy, even a puppy can do it!

concert

A concert is a time when musicians play for an audience.

Everyone dances at the Scat Cat Band **concert**.

cook

When you cook food, you heat it up by boiling, baking or frying it.

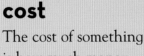

It's fun to **cook** outdoors over a fire!

costume

A costume is clothing you put on so that you will look like someone else.

When Mickey puts on this **costume**, he becomes the Sorcerer's Apprentice!

cookies

Cookies are round, sweet, baked snacks made with flour, sugar, butter and other things.

Look at all the yummy **cookies** on that plate!

corner

A corner is where two walls or two streets come together.

The cats ran around the **corner** when they smelled fresh milk!

corn

Corn is a vegetable with little rows of yellow seeds, that grows on a tall, green plant.

When **corn** is freshly picked, it still has green leaves on it.

cost

The cost of something is how much money it takes to buy it.

This one **costs** less!

cough

When you cough, you try to clear your throat.

What do you think is making Goofy cough?

cow

A cow is a large farm animal that moos.

Cows come in many different colours. Some of them even have spots.

crackers

Crackers are thin, crispy snacks made of flour and water.

Crackers and cheese taste good together.

count

You count things to find out how many of them you have.

Now stand still so I can count you all!

cowboy

A cowboy is someone who works on a ranch and rides a horse.

Woody is the best cowboy in the whole world!

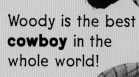

cricket

Cricket is a game played between two teams of eleven players. While one team tries to hit a ball with a bat to score "runs", the other team tries to get them out.

Let's play cricket!

cousin

Your cousin is the child of your aunt and uncle.

If Aunt Flora had a daughter, she would be Aurora's cousin.

crab

A crab is an animal that lives in the water. It has a shell, eight legs and two big claws.

Sebastian the crab is Ariel's friend.

crocodile

A crocodile is an animal that lives in salty water. It has short legs, tough skin and a long snout.

That crocodile has a lot of teeth to brush!

crown

A crown is a round thing made of metal and jewels that kings and queens wear on their heads.

Robin Hood thought the nicest thing about King John was his **crown**.

cup

A cup is a container with a handle, that you drink from.

Would you like a **cup** of tea?

cut

When you cut something, you use a knife or a pair of scissors to divide it into parts.

Gus and Jaq **cut** a long piece of ribbon for Cinderella's dress.

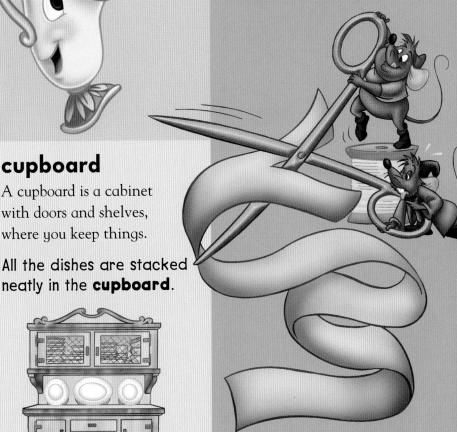

cry

When you cry, tears drip from your eyes because you are upset.

Daisy always **cries** at sad films.

cupboard

A cupboard is a cabinet with doors and shelves, where you keep things.

All the dishes are stacked neatly in the **cupboard**.

cucumber

A cucumber is a vegetable with seeds, usually eaten raw in salads.

The best way to eat a **cucumber** is in slices.

cushion

A cushion is a pillow on a chair or a sofa.

The **cushions** on the sofa are so soft!

cymbals

Cymbals are two big circles of metal that are banged together to make a loud musical sound.

Crash! The Scat Cat Band loves to play the **cymbals**.

Dd

dog

dancer

A dancer is someone who likes to move to music.

Donald is a surprisingly graceful **dancer**.

deer

A deer is an animal with four legs that lives in the forest. Young deer have spots on their fur.

This young **deer** is Bambi, the Prince of the Forest!

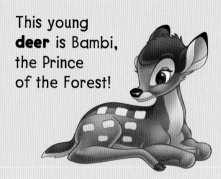

daughter

A daughter is a female child.

Mulan is the **daughter** in her family.

dentist

A dentist helps take care of your teeth.

A **dentist** uses a lot of tools to clean your teeth.

dance

When you dance, you move your body to music.

Belle and the Beast **dance** together beautifully.

day

A day is twenty-four hours long. Morning, afternoon and evening are all part of one day.

My favourite **day** is Saturday!

department store

A department store has several areas selling different things.

There are so many different things to buy in this **department store**!

A
B
C
D
E
F
G
H
I
J
K
L
M
N
O
P
Q
R
S
T
U
V
W
X
Y
Z

A
B
C
D
E
F
G
H
I
J
K
L
M
N
O
P
Q
R
S
T
U
V
W
X
Y
Z

desert

A desert is a very hot, sandy, dry place.

Aladdin doesn't like being in the **desert**, but his friend does!

dinner

Dinner is the last meal of the day.

Who invited them to **dinner**?

desk

A desk is a piece of furniture used for writing and other kinds of work.

You will do a lot of work at your **desk** in school.

different

If something is different, it is not like other things.

Ariel is **different** from her sisters.

dessert

Dessert is a sweet food, usually eaten after dinner.

Grab a spoon and dig into this delicious **dessert**!

difficult

If something is difficult, it is hard to do or to understand.

Minnie has just learned to play a very **difficult** piece of music.

direction

A direction is somewhere you look at or point to.

Is Geppetto in this **direction**?

dirty

When something is dirty, it is not clean.

It's fun to get **dirty**!

dishwasher

A dishwasher is a machine that washes dishes.

The **dishwasher** makes dirty dishes shiny and clean!

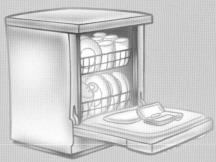

doctor

A doctor helps to make you better when you're sick.

This monster is pretending to be a **doctor**.

disagree

If you disagree with somebody, you each have different ideas about something.

I **disagree**! Baseball is more fun than chess!

diving

Diving is when you jump head first into a pool. It is also short for scuba diving, when you go deep underwater with a tank that helps you to breathe.

I'm **diving** in!

dog

A dog is a pet that barks and wags its tail when it's happy.

Lady and Tramp are two **dogs** in love.

dishes

Dishes are used to hold food.

Where do you keep the **dishes** in your house?

DJ

A DJ is someone who chooses music to play on the radio or at dance events.

Hey, **DJ**, pump up that tune!

doll

A doll is a toy that looks like a person.

A **doll** is always ready to be your friend!

dolphin

A dolphin is a very smart, small whale that lives in the sea and is friendly to people.

Dolphins like to swim with people. Would you like to swim with a **dolphin**?

drawer

A drawer is part of a piece of furniture that slides in and out and holds things.

You can keep your pyjamas in one **drawer** and your shirts in another.

door

You open and close a door to get in and out of a room or building.

What do you think is behind that **door**?

down

When something is down, it is in a low place.

Be very careful coming **down** the stairs!

dream

You dream stories while you are sleeping.

Donald **dreams** that Daisy is having a good time at the beach.

doorbell

A doorbell is outside a house. When you press it, it rings to let people know you are there.

Brrring! Ring the **doorbell** again to make sure Minnie knows we're here!

MINNIE

draw

When you draw, you make pictures with a pencil, pen, crayon or chalk.

Jane loves to **draw** everything in the jungle!

dress

A dress is a top and a skirt joined together as one piece and worn by girls and women.

Do you like my pink **dress**?

drive

When you are old enough to drive, you will be able to steer a machine like a car or truck.

Would you like to **drive** a taxi in Monstropolis?

drop

When you drop something, you let it fall.

Be careful not to **drop** your ice cream on the ground!

dry

When something is dry, it is not wet.

Ha! You think you'll ever **dry** off?

duck

A duck is a flying bird that quacks and likes to live and swim in water.

Ducks don't like to be chased by dogs!

drink

A drink is a liquid food like milk or water.

Pluto takes a **drink** of water in the hot afternoon.

drum

A drum is a round musical instrument that you bang on with sticks to make a sound.

The Scat Cat Band can really play those **drums**!

DVD

A DVD is a disc that enables you to watch a film or TV programme whenever you want on a DVD player or computer.

It's raining. Let's watch a **DVD**.

A B C D E F G H I J K L M N O P Q R S T U V W X Y Z

39

elephant

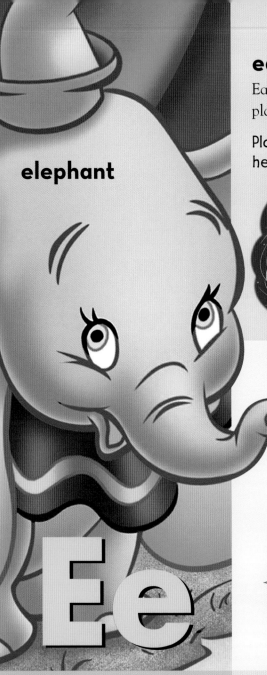

Ee

earth

Earth is the name of the planet you live on.

Planet **Earth** is out here somewhere!

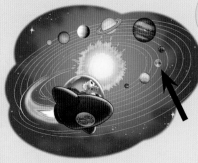

eat

When you eat, you take food into your mouth, then chew it and swallow it.

I can **eat** a lot of these!

east

East is the opposite direction of west.

The sun rises in the **east** each morning.

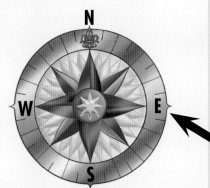

eggs

Eggs are oval objects in which baby animals develop until they are ready to be born. They often have shells.

All birds lay **eggs**.

early

Early means before the usual time.

Daisy is too **early** to buy her train ticket.

easy

If something is easy, it means it is not hard to do.

It's **easy** for Pluto to sing along to Goofy's music!

elephant

An elephant is a large animal with big ears and a long nose called a trunk.

An **elephant** raises its trunk when it's happy.

entrance

An entrance is the opening you go through to get inside a building.

Mickey goes through the **entrance** to meet Minnie.

environment

Your environment is everything around you, including the trees, the clouds and the animals.

We must look after our **environment**!

e-mail

E-mail is the kind of mail you get through your computer or smart phone.

Lilo sends an **e-mail** every day to her Elvis Fan Club.

escalator

An escalator is a moving stairway that takes you up or down from floor to floor.

Oh, no! This **escalator** leads to even more shops!

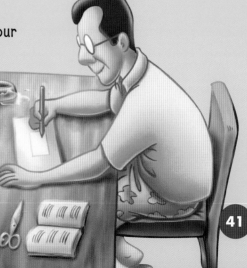

empty

Empty means that there is nothing inside.

Garsh! This is **empty** except for my socks!

envelope

An envelope is what you need to post a letter.

You need a stamp on your **envelope** before you post it.

A
B
C
D
E
F
G
H
I
J
K
L
M
N
O
P
Q
R
S
T
U
V
W
X
Y
Z

evening

Evening is the early part of the night.

This **evening** is going to be fun!

exit

An exit is the opening you pass through to leave a building.

Goofy goes through the **exit** to the roof garden.

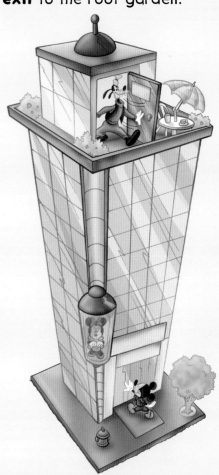

everyone

Everyone means everybody.

Everyone plays tug-of-war with the pillow!

excited

You feel excited when you are waiting for something or doing something that makes you happy.

Andy is **excited** about opening his birthday present.

everything

Everything means all things.

It's **everything** I could ever want!

exciting

Something is exciting when it feels good to think about it or do it.

We're on an **exciting** magic carpet ride!

explorer

An explorer is someone who goes to unknown places to find out what they are like.

Being an **explorer** is fun!

42

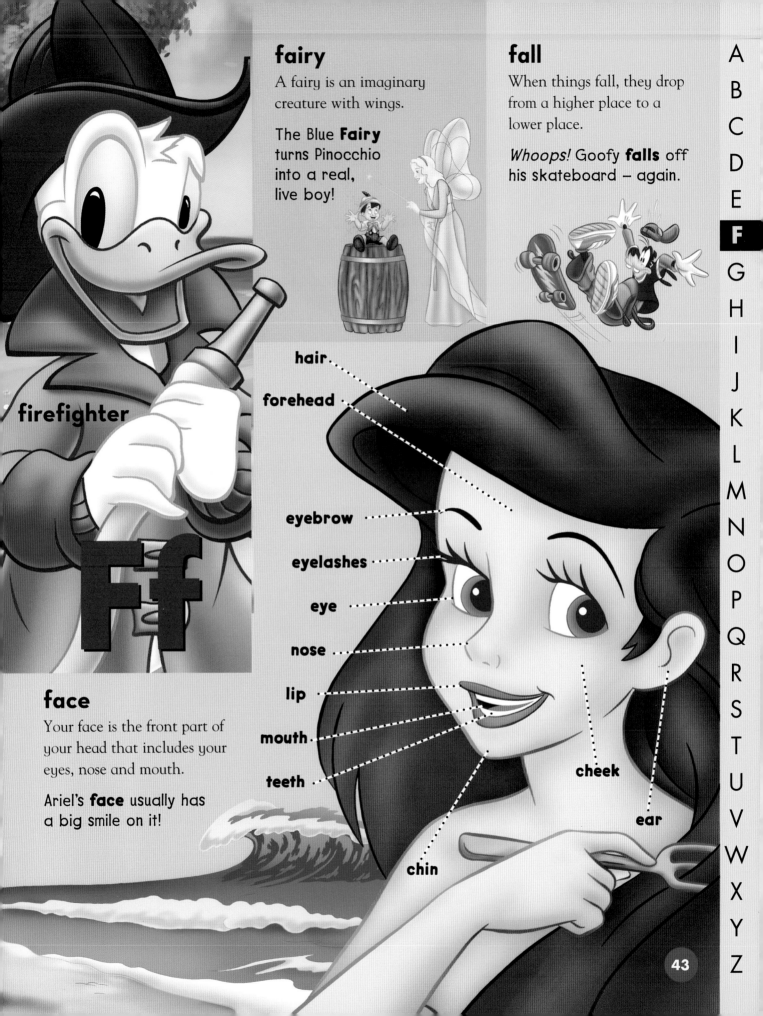

fairy

A fairy is an imaginary creature with wings.

The Blue **Fairy** turns Pinocchio into a real, live boy!

fall

When things fall, they drop from a higher place to a lower place.

Whoops! Goofy **falls** off his skateboard – again.

firefighter

Ff

face

Your face is the front part of your head that includes your eyes, nose and mouth.

Ariel's **face** usually has a big smile on it!

hair
forehead
eyebrow
eyelashes
eye
nose
lip
mouth
teeth
cheek
ear
chin

fan

A fan is a machine that moves air around to make you feel cooler.

Ahhh! That **fan** is a good thing on a hot day.

fast

When something is fast, it happens quickly.

Abu runs as **fast** as he can!

far

If something is far from you, it is a long distance away.

Simba is **far** ahead of Nala.

father

Your father is your parent who is a man.

I'll always be your **father**, Simba.

feather

A feather is a part of a bird that helps it fly and keeps it warm.

This bird's **feathers** are fluffy and white.

farmer

A farmer is someone who works on a farm.

That **farmer** is fast asleep!

feel

When you feel something, you touch it or it touches you.

Lady's fur **feels** so soft!

fence

A fence is a kind of outdoor wall separating two places.

This **fence** is between Donald's garden and his neighbour's garden.

fight

A fight is an argument between people.

Anastasia and Drizella are having yet another **fight** over Prince Charming.

fire

Fire describes the heat, flames and light that result when something burns.

Cowboys use an outdoor **fire** to keep warm.

fever

A fever is extra heat in the body when a person is sick.

The thermometer shows that Wendy Darling has a **fever**.

finish

To finish something is to come to the end of it.

Simba and Nala are about to **finish** their race.

firefighter

A firefighter is a person whose job it is to put out fires.

I'm proud to be a **firefighter**!

field

A field is a flat, open piece of land without buildings.

Bambi and Faline play in the **field** of flowers.

fireplace

A fireplace is the area where adults can build a safe fire to help warm up a room.

A **fireplace** helps a room feel warm and cosy.

A B C D E **F** G H I J K L M N O P Q R S T U V W X Y Z

fireworks

When lit, fireworks make loud noises and create beautiful, bright lights in the sky.

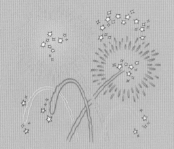

Fireworks are so colourful — and so loud!

fish

A fish is an animal with fins that lives in the water and breathes through gills.

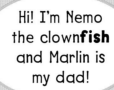

Hi! I'm Nemo the clown**fish** and Marlin is my dad!

first

When something comes first, it comes before anything else.

Doc is the **first** in the line of Dwarfs.

fishbowl

A fishbowl is a see-through container that holds water and pet fish.

A **fishbowl** home has lots of good views!

float

To float means to stay on top of the water and not sink.

This is the only way to **float**, Stitch!

first-aid kit

A first-aid kit is a container that holds things to treat an injury or sickness.

It's a good idea to have a **first-aid kit** in your house.

flag

A flag is a piece of cloth with a coloured design on it that stands for something.

Can you see the red **flag** flying on this green castle?

floor

A floor is the part of a room that you walk on.

Be careful — the **floor** is slippery!

florist

A florist is a person who sells flowers.

You can buy all sorts of pretty flowers from the **florist**.

flute

A flute is a musical instrument shaped like a long tube, which you hold sideways and play by blowing into a hole.

A **flute** can make high sounds.

fold

When you fold something, you bend one part over another.

Huey and Dewey **fold** their homework papers, and suddenly homework is more fun!

flour

Flour is a powder you use in baking.

Take two scoops of **flour** from that sack for the cake that we're making.

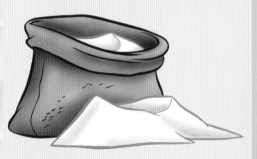

fly

A fly is an insect with one set of clear wings.

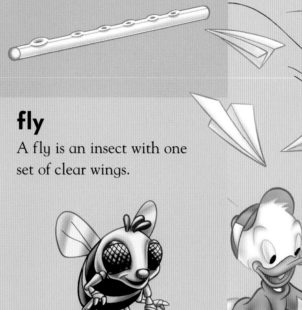

That **fly** is buzzing about, looking for food.

flower

A flower is the colourful part of a plant that has petals and contains seeds.

Flowers come in so many bright colours!

fly

To fly means to move through the air.

Zazu tries to **fly** out of Simba's reach.

follow

When you follow something, you go after it or behind it.

Follow me if you want an adventure!

A B C D E **F** G H I J K L M N O P Q R S T U V W X Y Z

A
B
C
D
E
F
G
H
I
J
K
L
M
N
O
P
Q
R
S
T
U
V
W
X
Y
Z

football

Football is a game played by two teams, where each team tries to kick the football into the other team's goal.

Mickey and Goofy like to play **football** together.

fork

A fork is a tool that you use when you eat. It has long, pointy parts and a handle.

You can use this **fork** to pick up your food.

free

Something is free if it costs nothing.

So, Pinocchio, do you think this candy is **free**?

footprint

A footprint is the mark that a foot or a shoe makes.

The lion's paws make big **footprints** in the sand!

fountain

A fountain is a jet of water that shoots up in the air and comes down in pretty streams.

This **fountain** is in the middle of a park.

freeze

Water freezes when it gets so cold that it turns to ice.

Brrr! The snow on Mushu's tail is starting to **freeze** him!

forget

When you forget something, you cannot remember it.

How could Donald **forget** his money?

fox

A fox is an animal with red fur, a pointy nose and a bushy tail. It hides in the woods.

This **fox** is good at hiding from trouble!

French fries

French fries are strips of potato deep-fried in oil. They're also known as chips.

French fries taste so good with ketchup!

frown

A frown is the look on a person's face when he or she is unhappy and the ends of the mouth turn down.

Don't **frown** at the camera, Stitch!

fur

Fur is the thick hair on many animals.

Fur comes in many colours such as grey, white and brown.

friend

A friend is someone you like and have fun with.

Woody is my best **friend**!

fruit

A fruit is something that grows on trees or plants, has seeds and is tasty to eat.

Fruit salad is delicious with ice cream.

furniture

Furniture is the objects you have to sit on and hold things in your house, such as tables, chairs, cupboards and beds.

Where should Mickey put this piece of **furniture**?

frog

A frog is a hopping animal with smooth skin that says "ribbit".

This **frog** lives in a pond.

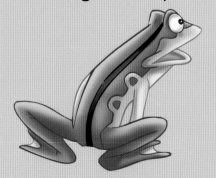

full

Full means that there is no room for anything more.

Minnie's refrigerator is **full** of good things to eat!

A
B
C
D
E
F
G
H
I
J
K
L
M
N
O
P
Q
R
S
T
U
V
W
X
Y
Z

A B C D E F **G** H I J K L M N O P Q R S T U V W X Y Z

grapes

Gg

garden

A garden is a spot where people grow flowers, vegetables and other plants.

> I water my **garden** to help it grow!

generous

If something is generous, it means that it is more than expected.

Robin Hood gave the poor rabbit a **generous** gift.

get

To get something is to have it by borrowing it, buying it or receiving it from someone else.

Pluto **gets** a special present!

garage

A garage is a building where one or more vehicles are parked.

Mickey parks his car in the **garage** when it rains.

genie

A genie usually lives in a magic lamp and can make wishes come true.

> Hiya, Al! Your personal **genie** here, at your service!

ghost

A ghost is thought to be the spirit of someone who has died.

A **ghost** says "boo!" to scare you!

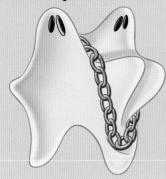

girl

A girl is a child who will grow up to become a woman.

Aloha! I'm a **girl** named Lilo. Who are you?

glasses

Glasses are frames with special glass in them that you wear over your eyes when you need to see better.

The eye doctor will tell you if you need **glasses**.

giraffe

A giraffe is a very tall, spotted animal with long, thin legs and a very long neck.

Because of its long neck, a **giraffe** can reach the leaves on the tallest trees.

give

When you give to someone, you let them have something.

Give the remote control to Roger! It's time to watch our favourite show!

glass

A glass is a container that we drink from.

This **glass** is half full.

globe

A globe is a round map of the world.

A **globe** can show you all the water and all the land on the Earth.

A B C D E F **G** H I J K L M N O P Q R S T U V W X Y Z

glove

A glove is a piece of clothing that covers each finger of your hand separately to keep you warm or clean.

You can wiggle your fingers in your glove!

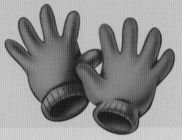

goal

In some sports, a goal is the place where you try to get the ball in order to score points.

Score! Donald kicked the ball into the **goal**!

glue

Glue is a gooey liquid that lets us stick one thing to another.

Glue can get very messy if you leave the cap off!

goldfish

A goldfish is a small, orange fish that many people keep as a pet.

Goldfish often live in a fish bowl or pond.

good

Something that we like or that is done well is good.

Abu is one of Aladdin's **good** friends.

go

To go means to move from one place to another.

When the lights turn green, the race cars go!

gorilla

A gorilla is a large and strong wild animal that comes from Africa.

This gorilla bangs on its chest to tell everyone it's here!

grandchildren

When you grow up, the children of your son or daughter will be your grandchildren.

Huey, Dewey and Louie are Grandma Duck's **grandchildren**!

grapefruit

A grapefruit is a big, round, juicy fruit that grows on a tree.

Some **grapefruit** are yellow and some are pink.

guess

When you guess something, you say what you think is the correct thing, but you aren't sure if it's the right answer.

Guess what's behind my back!

grandparent

Your grandparent is the parent of your parent.

This is Mulan and her **grandparent**, Grandmother Fa.

grapes

Grapes are small, round fruit that grow in bunches on a vine.

Do you like **grape** juice?

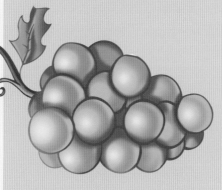

guitar

A guitar is a musical instrument played by plucking or strumming the strings with your fingers.

Rapunzel can play the **guitar**.

green beans

Green beans are also called runner beans or French beans. They are vegetables that grow in thin pods on a vine.

Fresh **green beans** snap when you break them!

gymnastics

Gymnastics are exercises that show how strong, bendy, well-balanced or fit you are.

Gymnasts tumble and spring and do amazing **gymnastics**.

A B C D E F **G** H I J K L M N O P Q R S T U V W X Y Z

A B C D E F G **H** I J K L M N O P Q R S T U V W X Y Z

hat

Hh

hairdresser

A hairdresser is a person who cuts and styles someone's hair.

A good **hairdresser** uses all his hands at once!

hairdryer

A hairdryer is a machine that dries your hair using hot air.

This **hairdryer** will dry your wet hair quickly.

hairbrush

A hairbrush is a brush that you use to make your hair neat.

Rapunzel brushes her long, golden hair with a **hairbrush**.

half

When you separate something into two equal parts, each part is one half of what you started with.

One **half** of the pizza looks as good as the other **half**!

ham

Ham is a kind of smoked meat.

Ham makes a good dinner with some fresh vegetables.

hamburger

A hamburger is made from minced meat, which is shaped into a flat circle and cooked.

What do you like on your **hamburger**?

hammer

A hammer is a tool you use to hit nails.

A carpenter always uses a **hammer** on the job.

handsome

A good-looking man is handsome.

Belle is in love with this **handsome** prince!

hard

Something is hard when it doesn't bend or change shape easily.

Call me Grumpy, but this bench is **hard**!

hang

When you hang something, you attach it at the top to something else.

After a hard day's work, the Dwarfs **hang** up their caps.

harmonica

A harmonica is a musical instrument with rows of tiny square holes that you blow into.

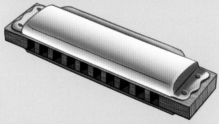

You play the **harmonica** by running it back and forth across your mouth.

hat

A hat is something you wear on your head.

Perla has a brand-new **hat** for spring!

happy

You are happy when you feel good about something.

Happy got his name because he's always **happy**!

harp

A harp is a large, heavy musical instrument that leans against you while you pluck the strings.

Duchess makes beautiful music on the **harp**.

hate

When you hate something, you really don't like it at all.

That crocodile really **hates** Captain Hook!

A B C D E F G **H** I J K L M N O P Q R S T U V W X Y Z

have

When you have something, it is with you, is part of you or belongs to you.

Snow White shouldn't have that apple!

heavy

When something is heavy, it is difficult to lift.

The small box is very heavy.

healthy

To be healthy means to feel well.

Running keeps me **healthy**!

helicopter

A helicopter is a flying machine with blades on the top.

You can see a lot of things down on the ground during a helicopter ride.

hen

A hen is a female chicken.

Hens live on farms and often have baby chicks with them.

hear

When you hear something, it means you listen to the sounds that reach your ears.

Thomas O'Malley likes to **hear** good music.

help

When you help someone, you do something to make things easier for that person.

I'll **help** you reach the food!

here

Here means in this place.

So many books! I think I like it **here**!

hide

To hide means to put something in a place where it cannot be found easily.

I'm good at playing **hide**-and-seek!

hike

To hike is to take a long walk, often out in nature.

The ants take Francis the ladybird on a **hike**.

hold

To hold something is to keep it in place.

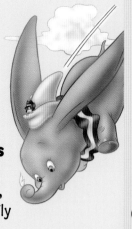

Dumbo **holds** tightly on to that feather, but he can fly without it!

high

Something that is high is far above something else.

Puppies love to jump **high**, especially for a treat!

hippopotamus

A hippopotamus is an African animal with a large body and short legs that spends a lot of time in water.

A **hippopotamus** can move around more easily in the water than on land.

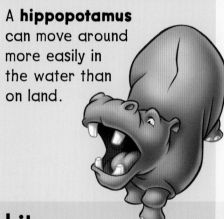

hole

A hole is an open space in something.

Gaston's big toe pokes through the **hole** in his sock.

hit

When you hit something, you strike it hard with something.

Oops! Louie didn't mean to **hit** Uncle Donald!

holiday

A holiday is when you take a trip away from home or school.

Holidays are a lot of fun!

A B C D E F G **H** I J K L M N O P Q R S T U V W X Y Z

home

A home is the place where someone lives.

Mickey lives in a very happy **home**.

roof

chimney

window

attic

hall

room

wall

stairs

garage

door

58

homework

Homework is schoolwork that you do at home.

Sometimes **homework** is difficult!

hope

When you hope for something, you wish for it.

Geppetto **hopes** for a son.

honey

Honey is a sticky, sweet syrup made by bees.

Honey tastes so good on bread!

horse

A horse is a large animal that neighs and has long legs, a long tail and hair on its neck called a mane.

Merida's **horse**, Angus, can run very fast.

hop

To hop is to jump.

Hop across to the other side, Bambi! You can do it!

hospital

A hospital is a place where people go when they are sick and need special care to get better.

A lot of doctors and nurses work in a **hospital**.

A B C D E F G **H** I J K L M N O P Q R S T U V W X Y Z

hot

Something hot is very warm.

The Genie likes **hot** summer days.

hot dog

A hot dog is a long, thin piece of spicy meat that you eat on a bun, often with mustard.

A **hot dog** is Huey's favourite kind of food!

hotel

A hotel is a big building with lots of bedrooms, where people stay overnight when they are travelling.

This **hotel** is in the middle of a busy city.

hour

An hour is a period of time, made up of sixty minutes. There are twenty-four hours in a day.

Sulley punches the time clock right at the beginning of the **hour**.

hug

When you hug someone, you put your arms around them.

Kala **hugs** her son, Tarzan.

hungry

When you are hungry, you need something to eat.

Dopey is very **hungry**!

hurry

When you hurry, you move fast because you want to get somewhere quickly.

Hurry! Catch that truck and it'll take us back home!

husband

A husband is a man who is married to a woman. She is called his wife.

Roger is Anita's **husband**.

ice cream

ice cream

Ice cream is a frozen dessert made of milk or cream, and sugar and flavourings such as chocolate or vanilla.

Mmmm! It's easy to finish **ice cream** before it melts!

ice skates

Ice skates are high shoes with blades on the bottom. You wear them to skate on ice.

These **ice skates** fit just right!

idea

An idea is a thought you have about something.

I have an **idea** about how to rescue Woody!

Ii

ice

Ice is frozen water.

The **ice** is kind of slippery, isn't it, Bambi?

A B C D E F G H **I** J K L M N O P Q R S T U V W X Y Z

A
B
C
D
E
F
G
H
I
J
K
L
M
N
O
P
Q
R
S
T
U
V
W
X
Y
Z

in

In means within or surrounded by.

Simba is **in** the cave.

internet

The internet is a worldwide network of computers that stores lots of information. When you want to find a website on your computer, you connect to the internet.

Let's look on the **internet** for that.

insect

An insect is an animal that usually has three pairs of legs and often two pairs of wings.

There are more **insects** in the world than any other animal.

iron

An iron is a triangle-shaped device that smoothes out the wrinkles in clothes using heat and steam.

Nani will have to use the **iron** on Lilo's shirt again.

interesting

When something is interesting, you want to know more about it.

Buzz thinks this rocket is so **interesting,** he wants to know how it works.

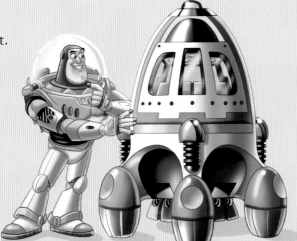

island

An island is a piece of land surrounded by water.

This **island** has a volcano!

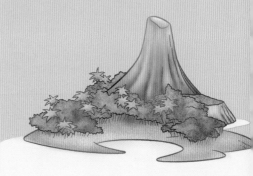

jacket

jam

Jam is a sweet food made from fruit and sugar. You spread it on bread.

What kind of jam do you like?

jar

A jar is a glass container with a lid that holds food and other things.

This jar will keep food fresh.

jewellery

Jewellery is the word for things people wear to decorate themselves, such as rings, bracelets and necklaces.

Look at Jasmine's pretty jewellery.

jigsaw puzzle

A jigsaw puzzle is a wooden or cardboard puzzle made up of pieces of a picture that have to be put together.

Whose face is that on the jigsaw puzzle?

jacket

A jacket is a kind of coat.

This **jacket** has a zip.

jeans

Jeans are trousers made with a type of cloth called denim.

Jeans are tough enough to wear in the playground.

joke

A joke is something that someone says to make you laugh.

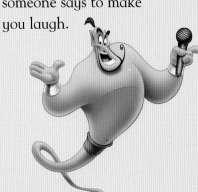

Genie tells a funny **joke**!

A B C D E F G H I **J** K L M N O P Q R S T U V W X Y Z

A
B
C
D
E
F
G
H
I
J
K
L
M
N
O
P
Q
R
S
T
U
V
W
X
Y
Z

juice

Juice is the liquid you get when you squeeze fruit or vegetables.

Apple **juice** is a drink made from apples.

jump

When you jump, you push with both your feet off the ground.

The Beast lands on his feet after he **jumps**.

jungle

A jungle is a warm place filled with trees, plants and wild animals.

Simba, Pumbaa and Timon eat grubs in the **jungle**!

kiss

Kk

keep

When you keep something, you hold on to it.

Lilo plans to **keep** Stitch forever.

kennel

A kennel is a house for a dog, usually found in the garden.

Here's a new **kennel** for my best pal!

keyboard

A keyboard is a long row of keys, either on a musical instrument or a computer.

A piano **keyboard** has eighty-eight keys.

kangaroo

A kangaroo is a jumping animal with big feet. The mother kangaroo carries her baby in a pouch in her belly.

Kangaroos come from Australia.

key

A key is a metal object that opens a lock.

This **key** fits into a special lock.

kick

When you kick, you deliver a strong, forceful motion with your foot or feet.

Ariel is so happy to have legs, she **kicks** them up in the air!

A B C D E F G H I J **K** L M N O P Q R S T U V W X Y Z

king

A king is a male ruler of a country.

King Stefan is Sleeping Beauty's father.

kitten

A kitten is a very young cat.

This **kitten** is sooo cute!

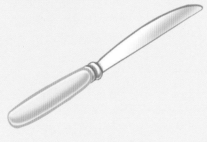

know

When you know something, you have learned about it and remember it.

I **know** that I should have listened to you, Jiminy.

kiss

A kiss is a touch you make with your lips.

Bo Peep gives Woody a **kiss** on his cheek.

knife

A knife is a tool for cutting many things.

This **knife** is good for spreading butter on bread.

kite

A kite is a toy made of wood, paper and string, which flies in the wind.

See how high in the sky that **kite** is flying!

knock

When you knock on something, you hit it to make a sound.

Snow White **knocks** on the door to the Dwarfs' cottage.

lion

lamp

A lamp gives off light and usually runs on electricity.

Turn on the **lamp** when the room gets dark.

late

Late means after the time something is supposed to happen.

I'm **late** for a very important date!

large

Large is another word for big.

Gus is a **large** mouse.

later

Later means at another time, but not now.

Robin Hood will give the money to the poor **later**.

ladder

A ladder is a long set of steps that you can move around and use to climb up high.

Each step of a **ladder** is called a rung.

last

The last one is the one that comes after all the others.

Dopey is the **last** Dwarf in the line. The turtle is the very **last** creature of all.

laugh

When you laugh, you make a special sound that means you find something funny.

Belle and the Beast share a **laugh**.

learn

When you learn something, you gain knowledge.

Students **learn** something new in school every day.

lazy

When you feel lazy, it means you don't feel like doing anything.

Donald is so **lazy**!

least

The least of something is the smallest part of it.

Baking is the **least** of Donald's talents.

left

Left is the opposite of right.

Simba is on the **left** side of the tree.

leaf

A leaf is the flat part of a plant that grows on the stem or branch.

This **leaf** fell from a tree in autumn.

leave

When you leave something, you go away from it.

Mike will **leave** his lunch box in the locker.

lemon

A lemon is a sour, yellow fruit that grows on a tree.

Sour **lemons** can be part of sweet lemonade – if you add lots of sugar!

less

Less means not as much as something else.

It takes Donald **less** time to fry an egg than to make a sandwich.

library

A library is a building with a lot of books you can borrow.

The **library** has many stories you can take home to read!

lifeguard

A lifeguard is a person who works at a pool or beach to make sure people swim safely.

A **lifeguard** must be a strong swimmer.

lesson

A lesson is something you learn that you didn't know before.

The monsters have a new **lesson** in scaring each week.

lift

To lift something means to pick it up.

Come on, Goofy – you can **lift** the suitcase! *Pull!*

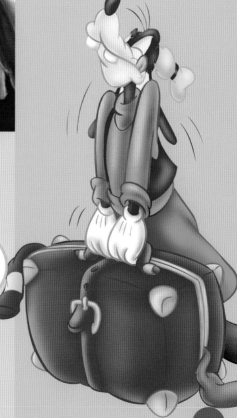

lettuce

Lettuce is a green vegetable with large leaves that you often eat as salad.

There are many different kinds of **lettuce**, such as iceberg and romaine.

lie

When people tell lies, they are saying something that is not true.

Pinocchio, don't **lie** to me. Tell me the truth. What happened?

A B C D E F G H I J K **L** M N O P Q R S T U V W X Y Z

lift

A lift is a little room that goes up and down in a building, taking people from floor to floor.

Minnie takes the **lift** to meet Mickey.

lightning

Lightning is the flash of light you see in the sky just before you hear thunder.

When it rained last night, there was a big bolt of **lightning** in the sky.

listen to

When you listen to something or someone, you pay attention.

Listen to me, Pinocchio. I can help you!

light

A light is a form of brightness.

Tinker Bell's **light** glows wherever she goes!

like

If you like something or someone, you feel good about them.

Meeko sure **likes** those biscuits!

live

To live means to be alive.

Donald **lives** the good life!

light

If something is light, it doesn't weigh very much at all.

The big box is **light** because it is full of feathers.

lion

A lion is a large wild cat that roars. The male lion has a mane of fur around his neck.

I'm Simba, and I've just become the **Lion** King!

living room

A living room is the room in a house where people spend a lot of time together.

Pluto watches his favourite film in Mickey's **living room**!

long

When something is long, the beginning is far away from the end.

Mulan's hair is **long**.

to lose

To lose is to be defeated in a game.

Pumbaa hates **to lose** every race he runs against Timon!

low

Something that is low is close to the ground.

Hooray! The bone is **low** enough to reach now!

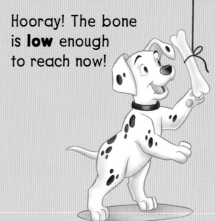

look at

When you look at something or someone, you pay attention to what you are seeing.

Mowgli **looks at** Kaa, and the snake puts a spell on him!

lost

If you don't know where you are, you are lost.

I can't be **lost**! The map must be wrong!

lunch

Lunch is the second meal of the day.

Donald needs a good **lunch** to get his energy back!

look for

When you look for something, it means you try to find it.

Help Turk **look for** Tarzan.

love

To love someone or something means you care a lot.

Sulley and his friend, Boo, **love** each other very much.

A B C D E F G H I J K **L** M N O P Q R S T U V W X Y Z

71

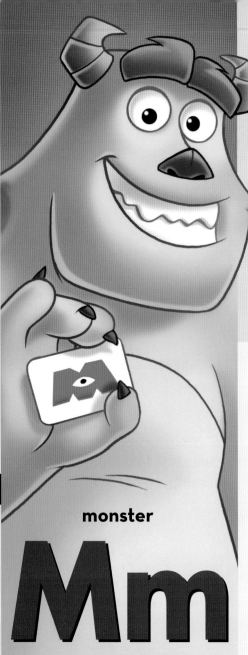

magazine

A magazine is something that you can buy to read, which has lots of colour pictures, news and interesting information.

There seems to be a **magazine** for everything!

magician

A magician is someone who performs magic.

This **magician** can do lots of tricks!

magic

Magic is the power to make impossible things happen, using charms or spells.

A little **magic** makes housework easier!

make

When you make something, you create it, put it together or change one thing into something else.

I can **make** a lot of things out of wood!

monster

Mm

machine

A machine is something built to do or make things.

Maurice's new **machine** is ready for testing!

man

A boy grows up to become a man.

Mr Darling is the **man** of the family.

map

A map is a picture that shows where places and things are.

This **map** shows the United States of America.

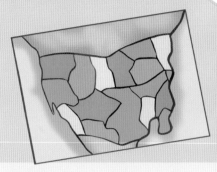

me

Me is another way besides "I" of referring to yourself.

Can you find **me**?

mean

Someone who is mean is usually unkind.

The Cheshire Cat annoys Alice, but he really isn't **mean** to her.

match

When two things match, they are the same.

Tweedledee and Tweedledum are a perfect **match**!

meal

A meal is the food you eat at one time. You have three meals a day: breakfast, lunch and dinner.

Wow! I've got three **meals** in one!

measure

When you measure something, you find out how tall or wide or deep it is.

Jiminy Cricket **measures** Pinocchio's *loooong* nose.

maths

Maths is learning about numbers, counting and doing sums.

I need to be good at **maths** to count all of you Dalmatians!

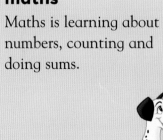

meat

Meat can be chicken, beef, turkey or pork.

This roasted **meat** is ready to serve.

A B C D E F G H I J K L **M** N O P Q R S T U V W X Y Z

medicine

Medicine is something people take when they are sick so that they can get better.

The doctor gives you **medicine** when you are sick.

melon

A melon is a big, ball-shaped fruit that is sweet and juicy inside.

A slice of fresh **melon** tastes good even if it's messy to eat!

menu

A menu is a list of choices.

There are so many delicious things on this **menu**.

meet

When two people or things come together, they meet.

I am honoured to **meet** you, Princess Jasmine!

melt

To melt means to go from being solid or frozen to being liquid.

Thumper drinks the snow as it **melts**.

mermaid

A mermaid is a girl or woman with human arms and a fishtail for legs, who lives in the sea.

Welcome to under the sea! I'm Ariel, the Little **Mermaid**!

merry-go-round

A merry-go-round is a ride where you sit on carved horses while the ride turns and plays music.

Do you like to ride the **merry-go-round**?

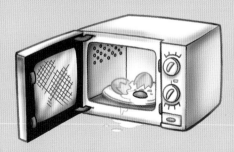

midnight

Midnight is 12 o'clock at night.

A new day starts one second after **midnight**.

mirror

A mirror is a kind of glass in which you can see yourself.

Look who's in the **mirror**!

microphone

A microphone is a machine that helps to record sounds or makes sounds louder.

A singer uses a **microphone**.

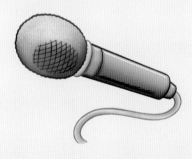

milk

Milk is what you drink to make your bones strong.

Slurp! It's fun to drink a **milk**shake!

miss

If you miss someone, you feel sad that you are not with that person.

Ariel **misses** Prince Eric.

microwave oven

A microwave oven cooks food faster than a regular oven.

It looks like Donald has been using the **microwave oven**!

minute

A minute is made up of sixty seconds. There are sixty minutes in an hour.

It only took a **minute** for Alice to fall down the rabbit hole!

mistake

You make a mistake when you do something wrong.

Whoa! Big **mistake**! These flippers have got to go.

A B C D E F G H I J K L **M** N O P Q R S T U V W X Y Z

mix

When you mix things, you put them together to make something new.

Snow White is **mixing** up something yummy.

monkey

A monkey is a furry animal with long legs and arms and usually a long tail.

Most **monkeys** like to eat bananas.

month

A year is broken up into twelve months. A month usually has 30 or 31 days.

March, April and May are all **months**.

mobile phone

A mobile phone is a phone you can carry and use anywhere.

Where's my mobile? Has anyone seen my **mobile phone**?

monster

A monster is an imaginary creature that is strange in size, shape and colour.

This **monster** needs lots of socks, shoes and gloves!

moon

A moon is something that moves around a planet.

Our **moon** lights up the night sky.

money

Money is the coins and notes you use to pay for the things you buy.

I have enough **money** for my big date with Celia!

morning

Morning is the early part of the day, before noon.

The Dwarfs go off to work every **morning**.

most

Most means the largest part of something.

Cinderella is the **most** beautiful girl at the ball.

museum

A museum is a building that contains interesting things for you to look at and learn about.

This **museum** has mummies on display!

mountain

A mountain is a very tall hill.

There's snow on that **mountain**!

mouse

A mouse is the object you move around to make things happen on your computer.

You need to move the **mouse** to make it work!

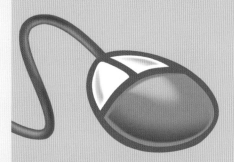

mushroom

A mushroom is a fungus that grows in dark, damp places.

Some **mushrooms** look like little umbrellas.

mouse

A mouse is a small grey or brown animal with long whiskers and a long tail. A mouse says "squeak! squeak!"

I'm the only **mouse** who can do this!

moustache

A moustache is hair that a man grows between his nose and lips.

King Triton has a long **moustache** and beard.

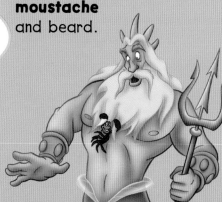

musician

A musician is someone who plays an instrument.

This Scat Cat is one good **musician**!

A B C D E F G H I J K L **M** N O P Q R S T U V W X Y Z

77

napkin

A napkin is a square piece of cloth or paper that you use to wipe your hands and face while you eat.

This pretty **napkin** is good for a fancy dinner party!

neighbour

A neighbour is someone who lives very close to you.

Hi, I'm your new **neighbour**!

near

Something that is near is close by.

Nala is **near** Simba.

nephew

Your nephew is the male child of your sister or brother.

Donald is glad only one **nephew** came to visit today!

newspaper

Nn

nails

Nails are thin pieces of metal, with a point at one end, that are hammered into wood to hold things together.

These **nails** can help Mickey build a new kennel for Pluto!

need

When you need something, you cannot do without it.

Mickey **needs** a towel!

net

A net is woven of rope or string and is used to divide, stop, catch or hold things.

This **net** divides the tennis court into two sides.

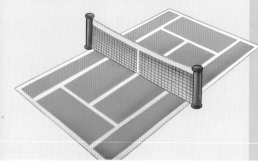

new

When something is new, it means that it has just been made or has never been used.

Daisy finds a good spot for her **new** vase.

nice

If someone or something is nice, it means you like them.

Sulley thinks that Boo is **nice**.

netball

This is a team game where players have to get a ball into a high net by throwing it to one another and then into the net.

This is the ball and net used in **netball**.

newspaper

A newspaper has all the news printed on big sheets of folded paper.

Tramp makes sure Jim Dear sees the **newspaper** right away.

niece

A niece is the female child of your sister or brother.

Daisy has three **nieces** named April, May and June.

never

Never means not ever or at no time.

Snow White has **never** seen so many dirty dishes!

next to

If you are next to someone, you are right beside that person.

I'm right **next to** you, Pumbaa, buddy!

A B C D E F G H I J K L M **N** O P Q R S T U V W X Y Z

79

night

Night is the dark time between evening and morning.

Night is the best time to tell stories around a campfire.

noise

A noise is a kind of sound, often an unpleasant one.

This drum makes as much **noise** as a Genie – almost!

no

When someone says no, that means they don't believe something, don't want to do something or disagree with something.

No! I can't go to the ball like this!

noon

Noon is the 12 o'clock hour during the day.

It's **noon**! Time for lunch!

north

North is the opposite direction of south. What is north of a place on a map is above it.

If you keep travelling **north**, you will reach the North Pole, a very cold place.

no one

No one means not anyone at all.

No one wants to just rest on a pillow!

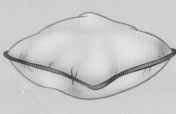
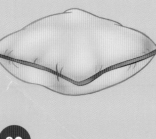

note

A note is a written way of saying something short.

Maid Marian finds a **note** from Robin Hood.

notebook

A notebook is a book with blank pages that you use for writing things down.

You can write your homework in this **notebook**.

nothing

Nothing means not anything at all.

Aladdin has a bunch of bananas, but Abu has **nothing**.

now

Now means at this time.

Simba is going to pounce – **now**!

numbers

Numbers are units used for counting and for doing sums.

Can you count the **numbers** from one to ten? How high can you count?

1

2

3

4

5

6

7

8

9

10

orange

oil

Oil is a thick, greasy liquid that does not mix with water. Some oil is used with machines, while other kinds of oil are used in cooking.

I use olive **oil** when I cook!

omelette

An omelette is made of fried eggs that are folded over and can hold a filling.

Do you like cheese in your **omelette**?

old

Something or someone old has been around for a long time.

Carl has to walk with a stick now that he's **old**.

on

When someone is on something, he or she is over and supported by the thing.

At last! I am **on** the throne!

octopus

An octopus is an animal with eight long arms that lives in the sea.

It takes a long time to shake hands with an **octopus**!

onion

An onion is a round vegetable that grows underground with a strong taste and smell.

Chopping an **onion** can bring tears toyour eyes!

ostrich

The ostrich is one of the few birds that does not fly, but it can run very fast.

An **ostrich** is the largest bird in the world, with a long neck and legs.

over

Over can mean above, on top of or finished.

> Watch me jump **over** you, Simba!

open

When something is closed, you open it to get inside.

Open the treasure chest to see what is inside!

out

When something is out, it is not in.

> Nala, why did you go **out** of the cave?

orange

An orange is a round, orange-coloured fruit with thick skin and a sweet taste, which grows on an orange tree.

Squeeze an **orange** and you get sweet juice!

oven

An oven is something you have in your kitchen that heats up and bakes food.

Mmmm! There's a freshly baked pie in the **oven**!

owl

An owl is a bird with large, round eyes. It says "hoo hoo!"

Most **owls** sleep during the day.

A B C D E F G H I J K L M N **O** P Q R S T U V W X Y Z

pyjamas

Pp

paint

When you paint something, such as a picture or a wall, you cover it with a coloured liquid, using a paintbrush.

It's fun to **paint**, isn't it, Berlioz?

paintbrush

A paintbrush is a brush used to paint something.

Paintbrushes come in many different sizes.

pair

A pair means two of a kind.

This is not a matching **pair** of socks!

page

A page is one sheet of printed paper within a book, magazine or newspaper.

Turn the **page,** and let's read the rest of the story.

painter

A painter is someone who paints.

I've always wanted to be a **painter**!

palace

A palace is a big and beautiful home for royalty, such as a king, queen, prince or princess.

Cinderella dreamed of going to the **palace**.

pan

A pan is a container people use for cooking.

Yum! Dinner is cooking in the **pan**!

paper

Paper is a thin material made from ground-up wood that is used for printing, writing, drawing, wrapping packages or other things.

The pages of books are made of paper!

parents

Parents are the mothers and fathers of children.

Aren't Wendy's parents a handsome couple?

panda

A panda is a large animal with black-and-white fur. It looks like a bear.

This **panda** had never seen anyone quite like Goofy!

park

A park is the grassy place where you go to enjoy being outside.

This **park** is a fun place to play in!

panther

A panther is a large, wild member of the cat family.

Some panthers are spotted, and some are all black.

parade

A parade is a group of people, including musicians, marching together down a street to celebrate something.

There's nothing like a **parade** in Agrabah!

A B C D E F G H I J K L M N O **P** Q R S T U V W X Y Z

85

parrot

A parrot is a bird with a hooked beak and bright feathers. Some parrots can talk.

What colours are this **parrot's** feathers?

pavement

A pavement is a cement path next to a street, for people to walk along.

Do you stand on the **pavement** and watch the cars go by?

peach

A peach is a round fruit with yellow and red skin that grows on a peach tree.

A **peach** is good in a pie, with ice cream, or all by itself!

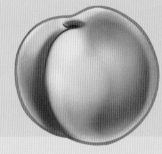

passengers

A passenger is someone riding in a car, bus, train, ship or aeroplane.

Miss Bianca and Bernard are **passengers** on a special flight!

paw

A paw is the hand or foot of some animals.

Simba swats at a butterfly with his **paw**!

pear

A pear is a bell-shaped fruit that grows on a pear tree.

When a **pear** is soft to the touch, it's ready to eat!

pasta

Pasta is a boiled food made of flour and water, often eaten with a sauce.

Lady and Tramp share a romantic **pasta** dinner.

pay

When you pay for something, you give somebody money so you can have it.

Stop right there! You have to **pay** for that apple!

peas

Peas are small, round, green vegetables that grow in little containers called pods.

Peas roll around on the plate so much, you need a spoon to eat them!

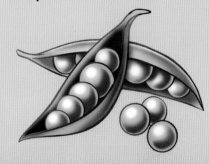

pen

A pen is something filled with ink and used for writing and drawing.

Belle picks up a quill **pen** to write a letter.

people

People are men, women and children.

These **people** (and dog!) make up the Darling family.

pepper

Pepper is a spice you use to flavour food. It is often used together with salt.

Achoo! If you breathe it in too deeply, **pepper** can make you sneeze!

pencil

A pencil has a coloured or grey centre and is used for writing and drawing.

You can rub out **pencil** lines.

pepper

A pepper is a vegetable that can have a mild or very hot taste and comes in many colours.

A red **pepper** tastes a little sweeter than a green pepper.

pet

A pet is an animal that lives with you and that you take care of.

Rajah, you're not just the best **pet** in the world — you're my best friend, too!

penguin

Penguins are black-and-white birds, most of which live in very cold places.

Penguins can't fly but they are good at waddling!

A B C D E F G H I J K L M N O **P** Q R S T U V W X Y Z

photograph

A photograph is a picture that you take by using a camera.

Who's in that **photograph**?

pick up

When you pick up something, you lift it up.

The animals show Aurora a few pieces of clothing they've **picked up** from the forest floor.

photographer

A photographer is someone who takes pictures.

Smile! I'm the Monstropolis **photographer**!

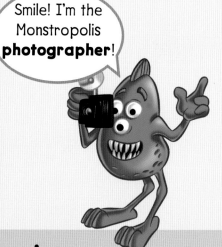

picnic

A picnic is a meal you have outdoors, often sitting on a rug spread on the ground.

Don't you just love a **picnic**?

piano

A piano is a large musical instrument with eighty-eight black-and-white keys.

You use two hands and even your feet to play the **piano**!

picture

You can make a picture by painting, drawing or photographing something or someone.

Can you draw a **picture** of a cow?

pie

A pie is a round, baked food with a crust and a filling.

Apple, lemon, peach and rhubarb are just a few yummy **pie** fillings. Which one do you like best?

pig

A pig is an animal with a fat body, short legs and curly tail. It says "oink, oink!"

A **pig** is a very clever animal.

pineapple

A pineapple is a large fruit with a thick skin and leaves, which grows in hot places.

Once you get inside the tough skin of a **pineapple**, you are rewarded with a sweet, juicy treat!

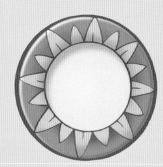

plate

A plate is a round, flat dish that food is served on.

This **plate** goes on the dinner table!

pillow

A pillow is a bag filled with something soft, such as feathers, that you rest your head on while you sleep.

The minute her head hits the **pillow**, Boo is fast asleep!

pirate

A pirate is someone who travels the seas to find ships to rob.

Aargh! Being a **pirate** is tough sometimes!

play

A play is a story that is acted out on a stage in front of an audience.

Lilo and Stich are the stars of their own **play**!

pilot

A pilot is someone who flies an aircraft.

Orville is both the **pilot** and the plane!

plant

A plant is any living thing that is not an animal. Plants grow in the ground.

Hello, little **plant**! I'm going to take good care of you!

play

To play means to do things just for the fun of it.

What do you like to **play**?

A B C D E F G H I J K L M N O **P** Q R S T U V W X Y Z

playground

A playground is an outdoor place with swings, slides and seesaws where you go to play.

I love to go on the swings at the **playground**.

pollution

Pollution is something that is harmful to the environment.

Pollution can be in the air and the sea.

plum

A plum is a fruit that grows on a plum tree.

Most **plums** are red or purple.

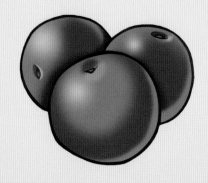

police officer

A police officer protects people from crimes.

All the **police officers** in Monstropolis are very good at their jobs!

pond

A pond is a small area of water in a garden or a park.

Fish, frogs and ducks like to live in a **pond**.

pocket

A pocket is a small cloth bag sewn into your clothing, used to carry small things.

You can keep spare change, tissues, keys and other things in a coat **pocket**.

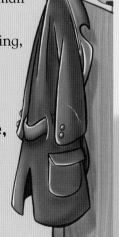

police station

A police station is where you go to report a crime.

The **police station** is filled with police officers.

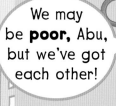
POLICE

poor

When someone is poor, it means that he or she has very little or no money.

We may be **poor**, Abu, but we've got each other!

A B C D E F G H I J K L M N O **P** Q R S T U V W X Y Z

popcorn

Popcorn is a snack food made from a kind of corn that puffs up when heated.

Popcorn can be sprinkled with salt or sugar, or coated with toffee. Yum!

postperson

A postperson is someone who delivers the mail.

Postperson Goofy is on the job!

pour

When you pour something, you make a liquid flow in a steady stream.

Here! Allow me to **pour** you some tea – make that tea for three!

poster

A poster is a very large piece of paper that you hang on a wall. It has pictures or information on it.

This is a **poster** of Daisy's favourite rock star!

pot

A pot is a deep container used for cooking.

Look at all the food in that **pot**!

post office

A post office is where people go to send packages and other mail and to buy postage stamps.

Let's go to the **post office** to buy stamps.

potato

A potato is a thick vegetable that grows underground.

Boiled, baked, mashed or fried, a **potato** tastes good!

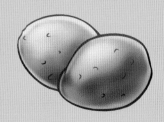

present

A present is a gift you give someone.

It's fun to guess what each **present** can be!

A
B
C
D
E
F
G
H
I
J
K
L
M
N
O
P
Q
R
S
T
U
V
W
X
Y
Z

91

price

The price of something is the amount of money it costs to buy it.

Sulley checks the **price** of a new lunch box.

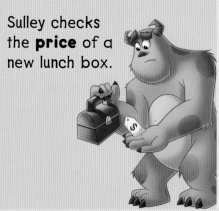

printer

A printer is something attached to your computer that prints out on paper what you see on the screen.

Most **printers** can print in colour as well as in black-and-white.

pudding

A pudding is a soft, cooked, sweet food, usually eaten after lunch or dinner.

Do you like chocolate or vanilla **pudding** better?

prince

A prince is the son of a sultan, king or queen.

Prince Phillip will do anything to save Sleeping Beauty!

pull

When you pull something, you tug it towards you.

Donald tries to **pull** the ladder down from the tree house.

princess

A princess is the daughter of a sultan, king or queen.

Princess Jasmine is the daughter of the Sultan of Agrabah.

problem

A problem is a difficult thing that you have to figure out how to solve.

Trying to walk on ice can be a **problem** for Bambi!

pumpkin

A pumpkin is a large, round, orange fruit that grows on a vine.

Cinderella's Fairy Godmother turns a **pumpkin** into a shiny new coach!

put

To put means to place something somewhere.

Daisy wants to **put** her own umbrella up in her garden!

puppet

A puppet is a kind of doll that moves. There are hand puppets and puppets with strings.

Don't forget, **puppet**, I am the boss!

purse

A purse is a small leather or fabric pouch in which people keep their money and bank cards.

Daisy keeps her money in her **purse**.

puppy

A puppy is a very young dog.

This **puppy** is always hungry!

push

When you push something, you press it with your hand to move it.

Mickey gives Ferdie a **push** on the swing.

pyjamas

Pyjamas are clothes that you sleep in that have a top and a bottom.

Comfy **pyjamas** help you have sweet dreams.

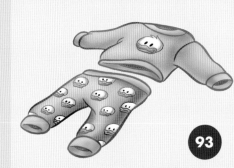

A B C D E F G H I J K L M N O **P** Q R S T U V W X Y Z

queen

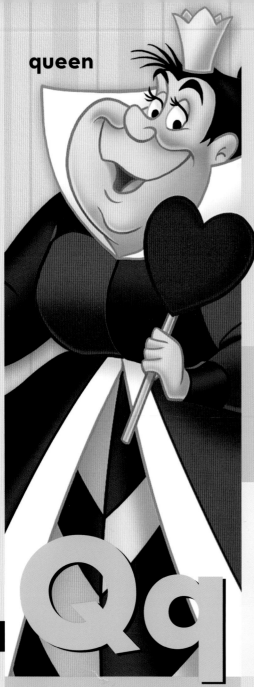

question

A question is something you ask when you need some information. When you ask a question, you want an answer.

So, Scuttle, here's a **question**. What is that thing?

quilt

A quilt is a cover for a bed. It has a soft filling inside, like goose feathers.

A **quilt** will keep you warm on cold nights!

queen

A queen is a female ruler of a country. The **Queen** of Hearts rules over Wonderland.

quick

Quick is another word for fast.

Donald has to be **quick** to catch those baseballs!

quarrel

A quarrel is when at least two people disagree about something.

Grumpy doesn't mean to **quarrel** with the other Dwarfs. He just can't help himself!

quiet

When something is quiet, there is little or no sound.

Princess Jasmine enjoys a **quiet** moment alone.

quiz

A quiz is a question-and-answer game where you are tested on what you know.

Clever Belle loves completing a **quiz**.

rope

race

A race is a contest to see who is fastest.

Let's **race** back to Pride Rock!

rainbow

A rainbow is the wide band of colours that sometimes stretches across the sky after it rains.

There's always a **rainbow** in Never Land!

radio

A radio is something that picks up broadcasts from radio stations so you can listen to what they are saying and the music they are playing.

Let's put some music on the **radio**.

rabbit

A rabbit is an animal with soft fur, long ears, big feet and a round, short tail.

This **rabbit's** name is Thumper.

rain

Rain is drops of water that fall from clouds.

Bambi gets wet from the spring **rain**.

reach

When you reach for something, you stretch your hand out towards it.

This little lamb is **reaching** out to play!

A B C D E F G H I J K L M N O P Q R S T U V W X Y Z

read

When you read, you look at words and understand what they mean.

I can **read** a good book for hours!

referee

A referee is someone who sees that the rules of a game are followed.

Stitch sits up high to be the **referee** at volleyball.

remember

When you remember something or someone, you have not forgotten that person or thing.

Donald can't **remember** where he put his key!

receipt

A receipt is a piece of paper that tells what you have bought and how much it cost.

Daisy has a large **receipt** from her last shopping trip!

refrigerator

A refrigerator is a machine that keeps food cold and fresh.

Let's look in the **refrigerator** for a snack!

remote control

A remote control lets you work something, such as a television set or a toy car, from a distance.

Does your TV's **remote control** get lost in the sofa cushions sometimes?

receive

When you receive something, it is given or delivered to you.

Donald **receives** a lot of bills in the mail!

relative

A relative is someone in your family.

The **relatives** in this family pose for a photo.

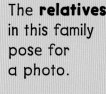

96

repair

You repair or fix something that is broken.

Would you let Goofy **repair** your table?

reporter

A reporter is a person who gathers news for a newspaper, magazine or radio or television station.

The Monstropolis TV **reporter** is on the air, giving the latest news.

restaurant

A restaurant is where people go to eat and pay for their meals.

I like everything to be perfect before I open my **restaurant**.

rhinoceros

A rhinoceros is a large animal with thick skin and one or two horns on its nose.

The rhinoceros is found in Africa and Asia.

ribbon

A ribbon is a long, thin strip of cloth, paper or plastic used to tie something together.

A present looks nicer with a pretty ribbon on it!

rice

Rice is a grain that is grown in warm, wet places.

Can you use chopsticks to eat rice?

rich

Someone who is rich has a lot of money.

I'm **rich, rich, rich**! And it's all mine!

ride

When you ride in or on something, you move along with it.

Stitch goes for one crazy ride!

right

Right is the opposite direction of left.

Nala, I am on your **right** side!

right

Right is also the opposite of wrong. If you do something the right way, you do it correctly.

That's the right answer! Very good work!

river

A river is a large stream of flowing water that moves from a high place, such as a mountain, to a lower place, such as the sea.

A river runs quietly next to Mickey's campsite.

rock

A rock is a hard piece of earth.

Rafiki presents baby Simba for the first time at Pride **Rock**!

ruler

A ruler is a long, flat piece of wood, metal or plastic that helps you measure the length of something.

A **ruler** can help you draw straight lines.

roll

When something rolls, it moves by turning over and over.

Sir Hiss **rolls** down the hill in his own way!

rope

Rope is a strong, thick string.

A **rope** can come in handy on a camping trip.

run

When you run, you move quickly, using your legs.

I'll **run** all the way home with you, Simba!

rooster

A rooster is a male chicken. He makes a loud cry when the sun comes up.

A **rooster** is also called a cockerel. It says "Cock-a-doodle-doo!"

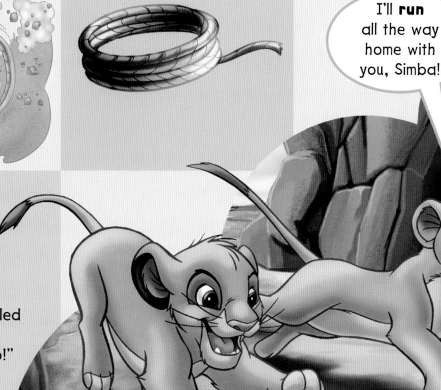

A
B
C
D
E
F
G
H
I
J
K
L
M
N
O
P
Q
R
S
T
U
V
W
X
Y
Z

shell

S s

saddle

A saddle is what you sit on when you ride a horse.

Riding Maximus would be painful without a **saddle**!

salt

Salt comes out of the ground or the sea and is added to food as a seasoning.

Salt is often kept in a **salt** shaker in the kitchen!

sail

When you sail, you ride on a boat that has sails.

Ariel watches Eric's ship **sail**.

sad

When a person is unhappy about something, he or she feels very sad.

Bashful is feeling **sad** because Snow White has been poisoned!

salad

A salad is a mixture of leaves, such as lettuce, vegetables and fruit that you eat cold.

Here's a crisp, fresh **salad**!

same

When something is the same as something else, it means that the things are alike.

Ha, ha! We're wearing the **same** dress!

sand

Sand is made of tiny pieces of rock and is found along the beach and in the desert.

*Uh-oh! So much **sand** and no Aladdin – and no banana!*

sandpit

A sandpit is a big outdoor box, filled with sand, that is fun to play in.

You can dig for hours in a **sandpit**.

saucer

A saucer is a small dish, made to hold a cup.

This **saucer** is a perfect fit for me!

sandals

Sandals are shoes with lots of open spaces to keep your feet cool in warm weather.

Your toes can wiggle "hello" to the sun when you wear **sandals**.

sandwich

A sandwich is two pieces of bread with some kind of filling.

What kind of **sandwich** do you like to eat?

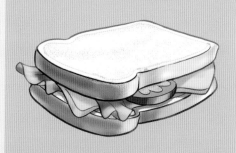

sausage

A sausage is a mixture of meat and spices, rolled up together.

Sausages taste good grilled or fried.

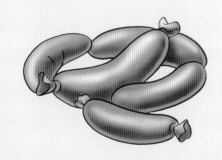

sandcastle

A sandcastle is a building you make out of sand.

Oh, no! Stitch is stomping on a **sandcastle!**

save

When you save something, you keep it because you want to have it later.

Huey, Dewey and Louie **save** money for Uncle Donald's birthday present.

A B C D E F G H I J K L M N O P Q R **S** T U V W X Y Z

saw

A saw is a long tool with many sharp teeth used to cut pieces of wood.

A **saw** can be used to cut down trees or cut up logs.

scarf

A scarf is a long piece of cloth, usually wool, that you wrap around your neck to keep warm.

The **scarf** is longer than the mouse!

scissors

A pair of scissors is a tool that people use to cut things.

You can use safety **scissors** to cut fun shapes out of paper.

saxophone

A saxophone is a musical instrument shaped like the letter S.

The Scat Cat Band always has a **saxophone** player!

scary

When something is scary, a person is afraid of it.

Everyone finds Ursula the sea witch **scary**!

scratch

When you scratch something, you rub it with something sharp, such as your fingernails.

Let me **scratch** that itch for you!

scared

If people are scared, it means they are afraid of something.

Sulley was **scared** when Boo pulled his tail.

school

School is where you go to learn many exciting new things.

Today's lesson in **school** is about shapes!

scream

When you scream, you make a very loud sound with your voice, without using words.

Some people **scream** when they see scary movies.

sea

Sea is another word for ocean.

Lilo and Stitch are almost ready to surf in the **sea**!

screen

The screen of your TV or computer is the glass part at the front that you look at.

Whose face is that on the **screen**?

seafood

Seafood includes all of the animals that live in water and that people eat.

Prawns, fish and lobster are all **seafood**.

seal

A seal is an animal that lives in and around the sea and uses flippers to move around.

This **seal** has a special talent!

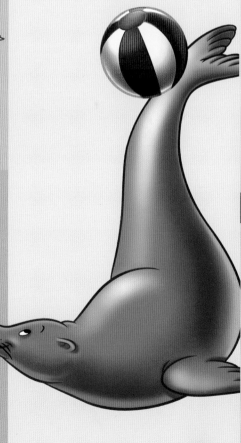

screwdriver

A screwdriver is a tool that pushes screws into wood.

Hold the **screwdriver** by the handle and turn it slowly.

seagull

A seagull is a large, white bird that lives near the sea, where it feeds on fish.

Now hear this! Scuttle the **seagull** has something to say!

A B C D E F G H I J K L M N O P Q R **S** T U V W X Y Z

A
B
C
D
E
F
G
H
I
J
K
L
M
N
O
P
Q
R
S
T
U
V
W
X
Y
Z

seasons

Seasons are the four different parts of the year called spring, summer, autumn and winter.

Which **season** do you like the best?

Spring

The **spring** rain tastes good!

Summer

I just love the flowers that bloom in the **summer**!

Autumn

It can be very windy in the **autumn**.

Winter

There's lots of slippery ice in **winter**!

second

There are sixty seconds in one minute.

Lilo counts the **seconds** she can hold her breath.

secret

A secret is something you don't want everyone to know.

Daisy whispers a **secret** in Donald's ear.

secretary

A secretary is someone who writes letters and keeps records for someone else.

A **secretary** works in an office.

see

When you look at something with your eyes, you can see it.

*I never thought I'd **see** this!*

send

When you send something, you make it go from one place to another.

*Let's **send** this far away!*

shake

When you shake something, you move it up and down or side to side very quickly.

Sebastian will **shake** anything to see if it makes music!

seed

A seed is the part of a fruit or flower that can grow into another plant.

Plant a **seed** and watch it grow!

sew

When someone sews, they join pieces of cloth together, using a needle and thread.

*Let's **sew** this bow onto Cinderella's dress!*

shampoo

Shampoo is liquid soap you use to wash your hair.

Shampoo has a fresh, clean smell.

sell

When you sell something, you let someone else have it for money.

Roger will never **sell** his puppies to Cruella De Vil!

shadow

When you stand in the sun, the dark shape your body makes on the ground is called your shadow.

Little John has a big **shadow**.

A B C D E F G H I J K L M N O P Q R **S** T U V W X Y Z

105

shapes

Shapes are what the outside of things look like.

Do you have a favourite **shape**?

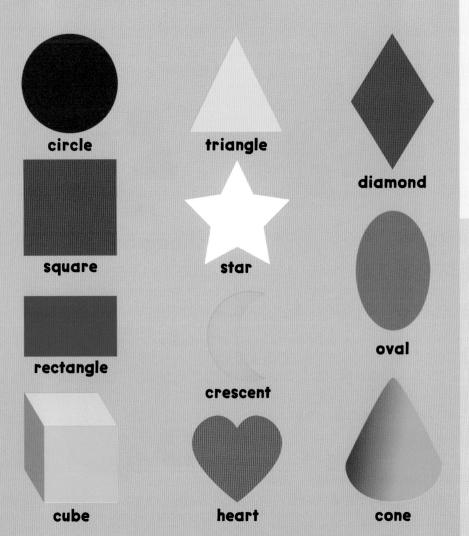

circle

triangle

diamond

square

star

rectangle

oval

crescent

cube

heart

cone

sharp

Something that is sharp has a pointed tip or an edge that can cut.

Captain Hook has a very **sharp** sword!

shave

When a man shaves, he uses a razor to trim the hair on his face.

Captain Hook lets Smee give him a **shave**.

share

When you share something, you give part of it to someone else.

Oliver and Tito **share** one side of the seesaw.

shark

A shark is a large fish with a big mouth and a fin on its back.

Look at the big teeth on this **shark**!

sheep

Sheep are animals with four legs and curly fur called wool. They say "baa, baa!"

Every spring, it's time to shave **sheep** for their wool.

shell

A shell is a hard covering that protects things like eggs, turtles, clams and nuts.

Ariel can find many pretty **shells** on the beach.

shirt

A shirt is an item of clothing with arms, a collar and buttons down the front.

Shirts are very smart.

sheet

A sheet is a thin, flat piece of cloth that covers your bed.

This bed has soft, white **sheets** and a blanket.

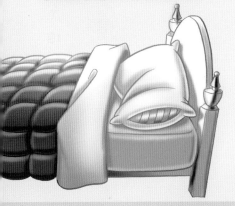

shine

If something shines, it gives off light.

The sun **shines** brightly on Daisy!

shoes

You wear shoes on your feet, over your socks.

Don't you just love my pink **shoes**?

shelf

A shelf is a place where you can put things.

What would you put on the **shelf**?

ship

A ship is a large boat.

This **ship** is going on a long trip.

shop

A shop is a place that sells things.

Let's go inside the **shop** and buy something!

107

A B C D E F G H I J K L M N O P Q R **S** T U V W X Y Z

short

Short means not long.

Alice is so **short**, she fits under the table.

show

When you show people something, you point it out to them.

Come on, Sulley. Just **show** me who you're hiding in there!

shorts

Shorts are trousers that only come as low as your knees.

Those are some fancy **shorts**!

shower

You stand under a shower to wash yourself with a steady stream of water.

Goofy sings in the **shower**.

shy

A shy person is someone who is quiet around other people.

Snow White doesn't mind that Bashful is **shy**.

shout

When someone shouts, they call out or yell in a very loud voice.

Timothy **shouts** to Dumbo!

shut

When you shut something, you close something that was open.

Sir Hiss thinks King John has **shut** the chest too quickly!

sign

A sign is writing, sometimes with pictures, that has information about something.

This **sign** shows the monster where the bus stop is.

sink

A sink is the bowl in your kitchen or bathroom that the water from the taps runs into.

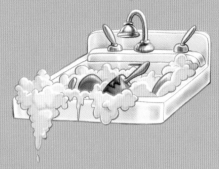

This **sink** is rather full!

skateboard

A skateboard is a long, flat board on wheels that you ride by pushing one foot along the ground.

When you learn to ride a **skateboard**, be sure to wear safety gear!

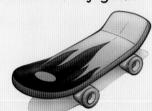

sing

When you sing, you make music with your voice.

Goofy **sings** his own special song!

sister

Your sister is the female child of your parents.

I'm glad you're my **sister**, Nani!

singer

A singer is a person who sings.

For a real **singer**, just call a Scat Cat!

sit

When you sit down, you are no longer standing up.

Belle **sits** down to read her favourite book.

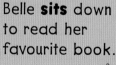

ski

To ski means to come down a hill on skis.

This is the first time the Beast is trying to **ski**.

109

A B C D E F G H I J K L M N O P Q R **S** T U V W X Y Z

skip

When you skip, you move by jumping and hopping along, one foot at a time.

Pinocchio **skips** off to school.

sky

The sky is what you see when you are outside and look up.

The night **sky** is full of stars.

sledge

A sledge is a flat board with blades under it that you sit on to ride down snowy hills.

A **sledge** can go really fast!

skirt

A skirt is a piece of clothing worn by girls and women that begins at the waist and falls around the legs.

This is a lovely **skirt** for spring.

skyscrapers

A skyscraper is a very tall building with many floors.

There are a lot of **skyscrapers** in this city.

skis

Skis are long, flat boards connected to shoes that people wear to ski.

Donald is not so good with **skis**!

sleep

When you sleep, you relax with your eyes closed, stop moving and thinking, and begin dreaming.

The Beast can **sleep** anywhere!

sleeping bag

A sleeping bag is a warm, padded bag that you zip yourself into when you're not sleeping in a bed.

A **sleeping bag** is cosy when you're camping!

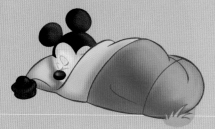

slow

Slow is the opposite of fast.

> Be glad I am **slow**, monkey!

smell

When you smell something, you use your nose to learn about it.

Minnie can't **smell** anything because she has a cold.

slide

A slide is something you slide down after you climb up a ladder.

Whee! It's fun to go down a **slide**!

smile

A smile occurs when you are happy and your mouth turns up at the corners.

> **Smile** for the camera!

slippers

Slippers are soft shoes that you wear at home, usually when you're in your pyjamas.

These **slippers** will keep your feet warm and snug!

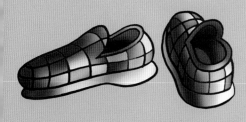

small

If something is small, it doesn't take up much space.

Abu doesn't like being so **small**.

smoke

Smoke is the cloud that rises from something burning.

Smoke is rising from that campfire.

A B C D E F G H I J K L M N O P Q R **S** T U V W X Y Z

snack

A snack is something you eat between meals.

Timon enjoys a crunchy **snack**!

snowball

A snowball is a round ball of snow, made to throw.

I'm going to win this **snowball** fight, Sulley!

snake

A snake is a long, thin animal that has no legs and slithers along the ground.

There are **snakes** in most of the countries in the world.

snow

Snow consists of white flakes of ice that sometimes fall from the clouds in cold weather.

Belle loves the falling **snow**.

sneeze

When you sneeze you make a noise as a lot of air suddenly comes out of your nose and mouth.

Achoo! Lumiere does a big **sneeze**!

snowboard

A snowboard is a flat piece of fibreglass or plastic that someone stands or sits on to slide down a snowy hill.

Donald can really balance on a **snowboard**!

snowflake

A snowflake is a single piece of snow. No two snowflakes are exactly alike.

Pluto leaps to catch a **snowflake**.

socks

Socks are clothing you wear on your feet, under your shoes. Socks come in pairs.

These **socks** match, so they can't belong to Goofy!

someone

Someone means somebody.

Someone is sleeping on the pillow.

snowman

A snowman is made out of big balls of snow.

Lumiere is melting the **snowman**!

sofa

A sofa is a long, soft piece of furniture that goes in your living room.

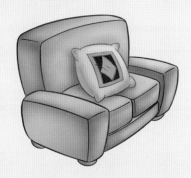

A **sofa** is a comfy place to sit and watch TV.

something

Something means some thing.

Pluto sees **something** he wants!

soap

Soap is what you use when you wash. It helps to make you clean.

That's a big bar of **soap**!

soft

When something is soft, it means it is not hard.

Grumpy wishes he had a **soft** pillow, too.

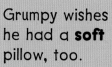

A
B
C
D
E
F
G
H
I
J
K
L
M
N
O
P
Q
R
S
T
U
V
W
X
Y
Z

son

A son is the male child of his parents.

Lady and Tramp have a son who looks like his father.

soon

If something is going to happen soon, it means it will happen a short time from now.

Mickey had better get here **soon**!

south

South is the direction that is the opposite of north.

The south is towards the bottom on a map.

spaceship

A spaceship is a machine, powered by a rocket motor, that travels into space from the Earth.

Lilo likes the spaceship ride more than Stitch does!

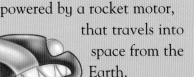

song

A song is music you make with your voice.

These are the notes of a beautiful song.

soup

Soup is a hot liquid food made with water or milk and other things, such as meat and vegetables.

Hot soup tastes so good on a cold winter's day.

spade

A spade is something with a handle and a scoop, used for digging.

It's good to have a bucket and spade on the beach.

spider

A spider is a small animal that has eight legs and spins webs.

Look at the **spider** hanging from its web!

spot

A spot is a small mark on something.

Look at all the **spots** on this puppy!

stable

A stable is a place where farm animals are kept.

Horses, cows, goats and other animals live in a **stable**.

spinach

Spinach is a dark green, leafy vegetable.

Spinach is good for you.

spring

Spring is one of the four seasons. In spring it rains a lot and flowers start to grow.

Goofy and Pluto love the **spring**.

spoon

A spoon has a little scoop at the end of a handle and is used for eating soft or wet things.

You eat soup with a **spoon**.

squirrel

A squirrel is a small, furry animal with a bushy tail, that lives in trees and eats nuts.

The **squirrels** are friends with Aurora.

stadium

A stadium is a large place with lots of seats around an area in the middle, where people go to watch sports or music events.

A **stadium** usually has no roof.

star

A star is a twinkling light, made up of gases, that you can see in the night sky.

Simba looks up at the **stars** when he thinks about his father, Mufasa.

stage

A stage is a raised area in a theatre where actors, musicians and dancers perform in front of an audience.

This **stage** even has palm trees!

stand

To stand means to be up on your feet.

Belle **stands** in her new dress and shoes.

stamp

A stamp is a small piece of paper that people stick on a letter or package in order to post it.

Make sure you put a **stamp** on your letter!

start

When you start something, you begin to do it.

We'll **start** eating dinner once you wash your hands!

stay

To stay somewhere means to remain there.

Stay home and have fun today!

stop

When you stop doing something, you don't do it anymore.

Stop the car, Goofy! It's the elephant's turn to cross!

steak

A steak is a slice of cooked beef.

Potatoes go well with **steak**.

storm

A storm is a kind of weather with rain or snow and usually a lot of wind.

Come, children. Let's get out of this **storm**!

storybook

A storybook is a children's book with words and pictures.

This **storybook** has lots of stories about magical people and places.

stepmother

A stepmother is a woman who marries your father if he's not still married to your mother.

Cinderella's wicked **stepmother** wants the Prince to marry one of her daughters.

stove

A stove is a machine that people use to cook food.

Who will clean up the mess on this **stove**?

A B C D E F G H I J K L M N O P Q R **S** T U V W X Y Z

strange

Something that is strange is unusual and different.

Even the Queen of Hearts thinks the Cheshire Cat is **strange**!

strawberry

A strawberry is a small, red fruit with lots of seeds. It grows close to the ground.

Fresh **strawberries** are so sweet and juicy!

string

String is a narrow rope.

String very often comes in a long roll.

street

A street is the paved road that cars drive along.

The cats chase Donald up the middle of the **street**!

straw

A straw is a long narrow paper or plastic tube that you use to drink something.

Suck in your cheeks when you drink through a **straw**!

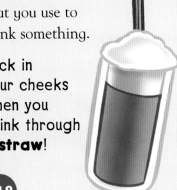

118

stretch

When you stretch, you spread your arms, legs and body out to full length.

Berlioz's nap is over when Toulouse decides to **stretch**!

stripe

A stripe is a line of colour.

The Cheshire Cat's fur is full of colourful **stripes**.

strong

If someone is strong, they have a lot of power.

I knew you were **strong** enough to hold all these books!

sugar

Sugar is a white or brown food that makes food taste sweeter.

Sugar comes in grains or cubes.

suit

A suit is a matching set of clothes such as trousers or a skirt paired with a jacket.

Look at this fancy, new **suit**!

summer

Summer is one of the four seasons. It is the hottest and sunniest.

The beach is great in **summer**!

sun

The sun is a star that sends light and heat to Earth.

The **sun** shines during the daytime.

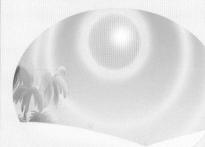

student

A student is someone who is learning something.

Mortie and Ferdie are **students** in Goofy's classroom.

suitcase

A suitcase is a container with a handle that people pack their clothes in when they travel.

This **suitcase** is jammed full of clothes!

sunbathing

Sunbathing means to stay out in the sun.

Nani spends her day off **sunbathing**.

A B C D E F G H I J K L M N O P Q R **S** T U V W X Y Z

sunglasses

Sunglasses are dark glasses that you wear to protect your eyes from too much sunshine.

Sunglasses are good to have at the beach.

sunrise

Sunrise is the time when the sun comes up in the morning.

At **sunrise**, Rafiki raises baby Simba up for all the animals to see.

sunset

Sunset is the time when the sun goes down.

Simba and Nala enjoy the **sunset** together.

sunshine

Sunshine is the light and heat that we get from the sun.

The **sunshine** is too strong even for a Genie today!

suntan lotion

Suntan lotion is a liquid you put on your skin to protect it from being burned by too much sunshine.

Before you sit in the sun, put on a lot of **suntan lotion**!

surfboard

A surfboard is a plastic board that people stand on while riding ocean waves.

You need to balance just right on a **surfboard**.

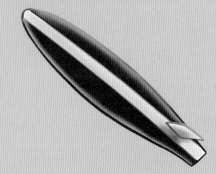

surfing

Surfing means to ride on a surfboard.

That guy sure is good at **surfing**!

surprised

If you are surprised by something, it means you weren't expecting it.

Cinderella is so surprised!

swim

When you swim, you move through the water, using your hands and feet.

I love to **swim**!

sweater

A sweater is a knitted piece of clothing you wear to keep warm.

This sweater is yellow and purple.

swimsuit

A swimsuit is the piece of clothing you wear when you go in the water.

Get your **swimsuit** and let's go swimming!

sword

A sword is a weapon with a handle attached to a long piece of metal with sharp edges.

I'll use this **sword** to slay Maleficent!

sweet

Something tastes sweet if it has sugar or honey in it.

Mickey gives a **sweet** heart to his sweetheart.

swing

A swing is a seat that swings from ropes. You sit on it and pump your legs up and down.

Mortie and Ferdie ride the **swings** in the park.

toothbrush

tablecloth

A tablecloth is a piece of cloth that covers a table.

Clarabelle doesn't want Horace to dirty the **tablecloth** when he makes his sandwich.

Tt

tail

A tail is something some animals grow at the lower end of their backs.

This monkey uses his **tail** like another hand!

talk

When you talk, you say words out loud.

Shh! Don't **talk**! Let me explain!

table

A table is a piece of furniture with a flat top and legs to hold it up.

The **table** is set for a romantic dinner.

take

To take something means to get it by reaching for it.

Baloo and Mowgli will **take** some bananas from the tree.

tall

When someone is tall, there is a long distance from his feet to his head.

How did Dopey get to be so **tall**?

tambourine

A tambourine is a round musical instrument you hit. It also has metal discs around the edges that jingle when you shake it.

Bang on the **tambourine** and then shake, shake, shake it!

tea

Tea is a hot liquid that people drink, made with water and the dried leaves of certain plants.

Some people like lemon in their **tea**.

tear

When something tears, it is pulled apart.

The crocodile waits for Captain Hook's coat to **tear**.

taste

When you taste something, you put it into your mouth to see what it's made of and whether you like it.

One **taste** and Genie realised it was packed with hot spices!

teacher

A teacher is someone who helps you learn new things.

Your **teacher** knows a lot of things!

taxi

A taxi is a car driven by a taxi driver, who people pay to drive them somewhere.

Most **taxis** have meters in them that tell you the fare.

teapot

A teapot is a container with a handle and a spout in which you make and serve tea.

I don't really mind being a **teapot,** love!

teddy bear

A teddy bear is a stuffed animal in the shape of a bear.

I sleep with my **teddy bear** every night!

A B C D E F G H I J K L M N O P Q R S **T** U V W X Y Z

123

A
B
C
D
E
F
G
H
I
J
K
L
M
N
O
P
Q
R
S
T
U
V
W
X
Y
Z

telephone

A telephone is a machine that lets you talk to someone who is not in the same place as you.

Brring! Brring! The **telephone** is ringing!

television

A television, or TV, picks up sounds and pictures that are broadcast for entertainment or information.

The puppies are gathered in front of the **television** to watch their favourite programme!

tell

When you tell someone something, you are sharing information that you know.

Tell me what to do, Grandmother Willow!

124

temper

If you have a temper, it means you have trouble controlling your anger.

Donald has a really bad **temper**.

tennis

Tennis is a game where players hit a tennis ball back and forth over a net with a tennis racket.

Minnie enjoys a good game of **tennis**.

tent

A tent is an outdoor shelter made of strong cloth and poles.

It's fun to sleep in a **tent** when you're camping.

test

When you take a test, you answer questions to show how well you know something.

Donald thinks the **test** is hard!

text message

A text is a written message you send and receive using a mobile phone.

Send me a **text message** to tell me when you're arriving.

thermometer

A thermometer is something that measures the temperature of a person or a place.

Can you read the **thermometer**?

think

When you think, you use your mind.

Aladdin **thinks** about Jasmine too much, according to Abu.

through

Through means from one end to the other.

Simba and Nala run **through** the valley.

thick

When something is thick, it is not thin.

One of you has a very **thick** tail!

thirsty

If you are thirsty, it means you need something to drink.

Timothy and Dumbo are very **thirsty**.

throw

When you throw something, you use your hands to make it fly through the air.

Roger **throws** a stick for his pal, Pongo.

thin

A thin person is someone who has very little fat on their body.

Aladdin is a **thin**, young man.

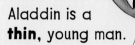

A B C D E F G H I J K L M N O P Q R S **T** U V W X Y Z

125

thunder

Thunder is the loud noise that comes from the sky soon after you see lightning.

The **thunder** scares Mike!

tidy

When you are tidy, it means that you are neat.

Lilo needs to **tidy**-up her room.

tie

To tie something means to hold it together.

You **tie** a tie around your neck!

time

Time is how long it takes for something to happen. Time is also the hours and minutes on a clock that show where you are in your day.

Oh, no! The **time** is midnight!

ticket

A ticket is a piece of paper that you buy in order to go somewhere.

You need a **ticket** for travel, too.

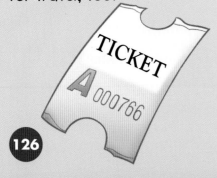

TICKET
A 000766

tiger

A tiger is the largest wild cat, with orange or white fur with dark stripes.

Tigers, like all cats, spend a lot of time sleeping, resting before the hunt.

tin

Tin is a metal that cans are made of.

This **tin** can holds tomatoes.

tired

You are tired if you are sleepy or need to rest.

When Timon is tired, he has a good place to rest!

toaster

A toaster is an electric machine that heats bread to turn it into toast.

This toaster can toast two slices of bread at one time.

toilet

A toilet is a bowl with water that you use to get rid of your body's waste and then flush.

You'll find the toilet in the bathroom!

tissues

Tissues are soft pieces of paper you use to wipe something with.

You wipe your nose with tissues when you have a cold.

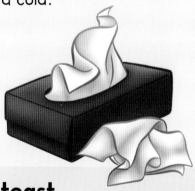

today

Today means this day.

Today is Mickey's birthday!

tomato

A tomato is a bright red fruit that grows on a vine and has seeds.

A sliced tomato is good in sandwiches and salads.

toast

Toast is bread that has been heated in a toaster until it is brown and crunchy.

Pop! The **toast** pops up when it's ready.

together

Together means with someone or something.

Boo, Sulley and Mike always have lots of fun **together**.

A
B
C
D
E
F
G
H
I
J
K
L
M
N
O
P
Q
R
S
T
U
V
W
X
Y
Z

A
B
C
D
E
F
G
H
I
J
K
L
M
N
O
P
Q
R
S
T
U
V
W
X
Y
Z

tomorrow

Tomorrow is the day after today.

Goodbye! I'll see you **tomorrow**!

toothbrush

You brush your teeth with a toothbrush.

Move your **toothbrush** up and down across your teeth.

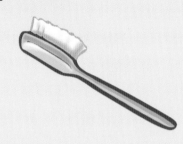

torch

A torch is an object with a bulb and batteries that makes a beam of light.

When you're in the dark, a **torch** can help you see in front of you.

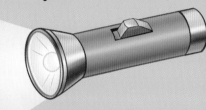

tonight

Tonight is this evening, the time that begins after the afternoon.

Tonight is for romance!

toothpaste

You put toothpaste on your toothbrush to help clean and polish your teeth.

Be sure to squeeze the **toothpaste** tube gently.

tortoise

A tortoise is a big turtle that lives on land and moves very slowly.

The **tortoise**, like all turtles, has a shell on its back.

touch

When you touch something, you use your hand to feel it.

No, Sleeping Beauty! Don't **touch** the spindle!

towel

A towel is a thick piece of cloth that you use to dry things.

This **towel** has lots of seashells on it.

toy box

You keep your favourite toys in a toy box.

This **toy box** is full!

traffic

Traffic means all of the cars, trucks, buses and other vehicles that are on the road at one time.

Oliver and Dodger find a way to avoid **traffic**!

tower

A tower is a very tall, thin building.

This castle has a lot of **towers**.

tractor

A tractor is a big machine used to pull farm machines or heavy loads.

This **tractor** helps a farmer with his chores.

traffic light

A traffic light lets people and traffic know when it's their turn to move and when to stop and wait.

toy

A toy is something you play with, such as a doll or ball.

The puppies share a **toy**.

Yup, the **traffic light** tells me I can cross now!

A B C D E F G H I J K L M N O P Q R S **T** U V W X Y Z

129

train

A train is a vehicle with an engine at the front, which pulls lots of carriages along a railway track.

This is an old-fashioned **train**!

trainers

Trainers are shoes with rubber bottoms and soft tops.

These **trainers** have laces.

treasure

Treasure is a collection of valuable things.

There's quite a lot of **treasure** in that chest!

tray

A tray is a flat piece of metal, wood or plastic on which you carry things.

You can carry a lot things on this **tray**!

That old buzzard won't find me in this **tree**!

REWARD

Robin Hood

tree

A tree is a large and very tall plant with deep roots, a trunk and branches.

trip

When you take a trip, you go somewhere else, for a holiday or for work.

Flik is taking a **trip** to the mountains.

trophy

A trophy is an award you get for doing well in some sport or other event.

This **trophy** is for the first-place winner!

trousers

Trousers are what you wear on the lower part of your body to cover your legs and bottom.

Trousers are made of cloth.

turn

When you turn something, you move it in a different direction or in a circle.

Flik **turns** his flying machine towards the enemy grasshoppers.

trombone

A trombone is a musical instrument made of brass. It has a part that slides up and down to make different sounds.

It helps to have long arms to play the **trombone**!

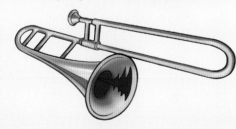

trumpet

A trumpet is a musical instrument made of brass, with only three keys.

Thomas O'Malley has heard enough of the **trumpet**!

twins

Twins are two people born at the same time to the same mother and father. Some twins look exactly alike.

Can you tell that we're **twins**?

A B C D E F G H I J K L M N O P Q R S **T** U V W X Y Z

131

umbrella

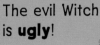

umbrella

An umbrella is a round piece of cloth on a handle that you open to keep rain from falling on you.

My **umbrella** is blue like a clear sky!

understand

If you understand something, you know what it means.

I don't **understand** these signs!

uncle

Your uncle is the brother of your father or mother.

Donald is the **uncle** of three noisy nephews!

uniform

A uniform is a special kind of clothing that shows what someone's job is, such as a police officer or firefighter.

This is a firefighter's **uniform**.

ugly

Something that is ugly is unpleasant to look at.

The evil Witch is **ugly**!

under

When something is under something else, it is below it.

Simba is **under** Nala.

up

When something goes up, it goes from a lower to a higher place.

Mickey and Goofy get **up** from the sofa to cheer!

violin

vet

A vet is a doctor who takes care of animals.

It can be rewarding but tough to be a **vet**!

visit

When you visit, you go somewhere to see someone.

Uncle Scrooge has come to **visit** Donald.

video game

A video game is a game you play on a special video game player.

Vanellope is a character in a **video game** called Sugar Rush!

voice

Your voice is the sound of you talking and singing.

The birds love Cinderella's **voice**.

vegetable

A vegetable is a plant or part of a plant that you can eat. Cabbage, beans and carrots are vegetables.

There's nothing like a crunchy **vegetable** for dinner!

violin

A violin is a musical instrument with four strings that you play with a bow.

Every orchestra has **violins**.

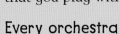

volleyball

Volleyball is a game played by two teams where each team hits a ball over a net with their hands.

Slam! The ball goes over the **volleyball** net!

A B C D E F G H I J K L M N O P Q R S T U **V** W X Y Z

A B C D E F G H I J K L M N O P Q R S T U V **W** X Y Z

woman

Ww

waiter

A waiter takes your order and serves you your meal in a restaurant.

Would you like Goofy to be your **waiter**?

wake up

When you wake up, you are no longer asleep.

Time to **wake up**, Belle!

wallet

A wallet is a flat, folded container in which you keep money, photographs and other things.

Tuck your home address into your **wallet**.

walk

When you walk, you move by placing one foot in front of the other.

I'd love to take a **walk** with you!

want

If you want something, you would like to have it. If you want to do something, you would like to do it.

I **want** that lamp!

washing machine

A washing machine uses water and electricity to wash clothes.

A **washing machine** is good for clothes, not trucks, silly!

water

When you water a plant or a lawn, you pour water on it to help it grow.

Cinderella **waters** her pretty little plants.

wardrobe

A wardrobe is a big cabinet that holds clothing.

Daisy has a very full **wardrobe**.

watch

A watch is a small clock you wear around your wrist.

Check your **watch** to see what time it is now.

waterfall

A waterfall is a wide stream of water that falls from a high to a low place.

Whoosh! You can hear the water rushing down a **waterfall**.

wash

When you wash something, you use water, and maybe soap, to clean it.

The animals watch Snow White **wash** her clothes.

water

Water is the clear liquid that comes from rain, melting snow or oceans, rivers and lakes.

Ariel just loves the **water**!

Left margin: A B C D E F G H I J K L M N O P Q R S T U V **W** X Y Z

watermelon

A watermelon is a large fruit with a green peel and juicy, red insides with lots of seeds.

Yum! **Watermelon** is a sweet summer snack.

wear

To wear something means to be dressed in some sort of clothing.

 I always **wear** fur!

weigh

How much things weigh means how heavy or light they are.

Daisy cannot believe she **weighs** that much!

wave

When you wave at someone, you move your hand to say hello or goodbye.

Lilo **waves** when she's happy to see someone.

week

A week is seven days – Monday, Tuesday, Wednesday, Thursday, Friday, Saturday and Sunday.

Next **week** we are going on holiday.

west

West is the direction that is the opposite of east. On a map, west is on the left side.

The sun sets in the **west**.

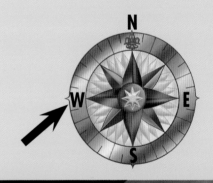

weak

Weak means not strong.

Donald is too **weak** to carry all that money.

weekend

Saturday and Sunday are the weekend.

Snow White bakes a special pie for the **weekend**.

wet

When something is wet, it means it has water in it or on it.

Ha! Rajah, you look so funny when you're all **wet**!

whole

If something is whole, it means it is all there and that none of it is missing.

Do you think you could eat a **whole** pizza?

whale

A whale is the largest animal that lives in the sea.

A **whale** comes up to the surface to breathe air.

wide

If something is wide, it takes up a lot of space from side to side.

Sorry, Pumbaa, but it's not **wide** enough!

whisper

When you whisper, you talk in a very quiet voice, so that only the person you are talking to can hear you.

Can you hear Belle **whisper** to the Beast?

whistle

A whistle is a small instrument that makes a loud sound when you put it in your mouth and blow in it.

Fweet! Fweet!
That **whistle** is loud!

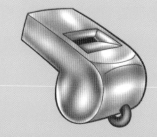

wife

A wife is a woman who is married.

Fa Li is the **wife** of Fa Zhou.

A
B
C
D
E
F
G
H
I
J
K
L
M
N
O
P
Q
R
S
T
U
V
W
X
Y
Z

win

When you win a contest or a game, it means that you come in first.

It looks like they both **win** something!

wolf

A wolf is a wild animal that looks like a large dog and howls in the night.

This **wolf** is looking for the Three Little Pigs.

wind

Wind is air that you can feel when it is moving fast.

Pocahontas loves the feel of the **wind** going through her hair.

wing

A wing is the part of a bird or aeroplane that helps it to fly.

A bird flaps its **wings** – then up it goes!

woman

A girl becomes a woman.

Aurora is a beautiful young **woman**.

winter

Winter is one of the four seasons. It is when it is the coldest and has the shortest days.

Goofy loves to make snowballs in **winter**!

wood

Wood is something you build things with, and it comes from the trunk and branches of a tree.

This table is made from planks of **wood**.

work

Work is the kind of job you do.

We love our **work**!

writer

A writer is a person whose job it is to make up stories or give you information by using words.

Belle wants to be a **writer** of great books.

worst

Worst is the opposite of best.

Pumbaa thinks rain is the **worst** kind of weather.

wrong

If something is wrong, it is not correct.

Without a doubt, this is the **wrong** foot.

write

When you write, you put down words on paper.

Mulan **writes** a letter to her grandmother.

A B C D E F G H I J K L M N O P Q R S T U V **W** X Y Z

A B C D E F G H I J K L M N O P Q R S T U V W **X Y Z**

X-ray

yoghurt

zip

Xx Yy Zz

X-ray
An X-ray is a photograph of the inside of someone's body.

This **X-ray** shows how bones fit together.

xylophone
A xylophone is a musical instrument made of strips of metal that you hit to make different sounds.

Here's an under-the-sea **xylophone**!

yawn
You yawn when you are sleepy by opening your mouth wide and slowly breathing in and out.

Sometimes you might **yawn** when you're bored.

year

A year is 365 days or 52 weeks or 12 months long.

January is the first month of a new **year**.

yoghurt

Yoghurt is a soft food made from milk that comes in many flavours.

Yoghurt is a good, yummy, quick snack.

zero

Zero is the number for nothing.

Zero comes before one.

yes

When you say yes, it means you agree with something.

Yes! I will fight Maleficent!

young

When someone is young, it means they have not been alive for a long time.

Even when he was **young**, Arthur prepared to be king.

zip

A zip has two rows of metal or plastic teeth that fit together when the zip is closed and come apart when it is open.

This new winter jacket has a shiny **zip**.

yesterday

Yesterday was the day just before today.

The rainstorm **yesterday** left puddles on the ground.

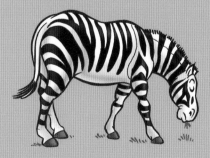

zebra

A zebra is a wild animal that looks like a horse with black-and-white stripes.

Zebras come from Africa.

zoo

A zoo is a place you can visit where all kinds of wild animals live and are taken care of.

Look what's happening at the **zoo**!

A B C D E F G H I J K L M N O P Q R S T U V W X Y Z

Mix

Sun

Lakes

King

Monkey

Queen

Snail

Grapefru

Ladder

Never

P

ig

Bat

Ostrich

Hop

Net

Zebra

Gymnastics

Cauliflower

Envelope

Apple

Fox

Notebook

B

Cat

Fores

Bir

Bee

Goldfis